THE LATE, GREAT
PENNSYLVANIA STATION

THE LATE, GREAT
PENNSYLVANIA STATION

BY LORRAINE B. DIEHL

FOREWORD BY
ADA LOUISE HUXTABLE

Four Walls Eight Windows
New York/London

© 1985 by Lorraine B. Diehl
Foreword © 1966, 1996 by Ada Louise Huxtable

Published in the United States by
Four Walls Eight Windows
39 West 14th Street
New York, NY 10011

U.K. offices:
Four Walls Eight Windows/Turnaround
27 Horsell Road London, N5 1XL, England

First cloth edition American Heritage Press 1985.
First paper edition The Stephen Green Press 1987.
First Four Walls Eight Windows paper edition 1996.

Acknowledgements of permission to reprint extended excerpts
will be found on p. 162.

LIBRARY OF CONGRESS CATALOGING-IN-PUBLICATION DATA:

Diehl, Lorraine B., 1940-
The late, great Pennsylvania Station / by Lorraine B. Diehl;
foreword by Ada Louise Huxtable.
1st Four Walls Eight Windows pbk. ed.
p.   cm.
Originally published : New York : Amerian Heritage, c.1985.
Includes bibliographical references and index.
ISBN 1-56858-060-6 (pbk.)
1. Pennsylvania Station (New York, N.Y.)—History. 2. McKim, Mead & White. 3.
New York (N.Y.)—Building, structures, etc.
I. Title.
NA6313.N4D5 1996
725'.31'097471—dc20   96-21056
CIP

10 9 8 7 6 5 4 3

Printed in the United States

FOR BILL

AND FOR SUZANNE

CONTENTS

The eastern facade of Pennsylvania Station, December 4, 1909.

FOREWORD

Pennsylvania Station succumbed to progress at the age of fifty-six, after a lingering decline. The building's facade was shorn of its eagles and ornament. The last wall went not with a bang, or a whimper, but to the computerized clack of leveraged cash flow computations. The passing of Penn Station was more than the end of a landmark; it confirmed the priority of real estate values over preservation. It marked the demise of an age of opulent elegance, of conspicuous, magnificent spaces, rich and enduring materials, the monumental civic gesture and extravagant expenditure for symbolic and aesthetic ends. Obsolescence is not limited to land use and building function in New York.

It was still the Gilded Age in 1910 when the building was completed by McKim, Mead and White, one of the turn of the century's most gilt-edged architectural firms. There was plush in the Pullman cars, crisp damask in the diners, silver bud vases on tables, and the New York-bound traveler debouched into a Roman tepidarium. Modeled after the warm room of the Baths of Carcalla, the station's main waiting room was longer than the nave of St. Peter's in Rome. Its vaulted ceilings were 150 feet high, and its grand staircase was forty feet wide.

The soot-stained travertine of the interiors, reputed to be the first used in this country, was from quarries in Tivoli employed in building the Eternal City. Its mellow, golden-cream was used in the Colosseum in the first century A.D. and St. Peter's fifteen centuries later. Six murals by Jules Guérin, huge topographical maps of Pennsy territory in sky blues, pale browns, and yellows, high in the reaches of the massive walls, gradually disappeared under layers of the same soot. Generous deposits turned the exterior Massachusetts granite from warm pink to dingy gray. Eventually, marble pomp was reduced to rubble, stone to dust. New York could be called the Mortal Metropolis.

Today's traveler, fed on frozen flight dinners from plastic trays, no longer enters the city in Roman splendor; the sense and ceremony of arrival has been replaced by the interchangeable fluorescent limbo of airports everywhere. At best, one comes through the bowels of a streamlined bird by the

Detail from an architectural drawing
of the station's main waiting room.

architect Eero Saarinen at TWA's Kennedy International Terminal in New York (also a landmark), where classical columns have been replaced by catenary curves. Architects' conceits may change, but businessmen remain the same; it is worth noting that Alexander Cassatt, an extremely astute investor and head of the Pennsylvania Railroad when the station was designed, wanted to build a hotel on the valuable air rights over the terminal. His architect dissuaded him, arguing that the railroad owed the city a "thoroughly and distinctly monumental gateway." As Lewis Mumford later observed, "Professional and civic pride won out over cupidity."

It was a shaky victory that lasted only fifty years—a moment in municipal time. A solid symbolic gateway was carted to the scrap heap, and the replacement, the thoroughly and distinctly mundane Madison Square Garden sports and entertainment complex connected to a twenty-nine-story office building, has already been declared obsolete. The "new" Penn Station lies buried beneath the complex; land values and air rights pushed it completely underground. The style is not Roman Imperial but Investment Modern—an aesthetic of expediency that gives a great return on borrowed money, but no return to society at all. It is a style, or non-style, that characterizes not only our common commercial construction but also the institutions and public buildings that were once meant to symbolize the shaky nobility of man. It is as common in New York today as the four orders were in Rome.

The station's decline began long before demolition. As time passed and grime gathered, life and architecture became noticeably less grand. The Great Depression made the once elegant terminal a home for the homeless, its increasing shabbiness and sense of inert time and the stale chill of hopeless winter nights immortalized by William Faulkner when he wrote: "In the rotunda, where the people appeared as small and intent as ants, the smell and sense of snow still lingered, though high now among the steel girders, spent and vitiated and filled with a weary and ceaseless murmuring, like the voices of pilgrims upon the infinite plain, like the voices of all the travelers who have ever passed through. . . ."

9

The concourse

With the return of prosperity, and the traveler, demolition by commercialization began. Colored ads appeared like blasphemous utterances in the marbled halls; automobiles revolved on turntables; shops and stands were added in jazzy cacophony. In 1958 a huge, lighted plastic clamshell was hung on wires from the Corinthian columns, hovering over a sawtooth arrangement of new ticket booths. The result, according to Mumford, was sabotage, a "masterpiece of architectural and visual incongruity." By 1963, when a group of prominent architects and citizens picketed the building to protest the announcement of the decision to demolish, it was hard to realize, with Philip Johnson, "that man can build nobly," in the light of the aesthetic debris.

Penn Station's great spaces and superb materials were genuinely noble, in a sense that architecture can no longer afford, in cubic costs alone. And the concept was noble, in a sense that society now tragically undervalues. In 1906, when the $25 million hole was dug in the old Tenderloin district for the $112 million terminal and landmark, the city's and the railroad's sights were high. After a few short decades, the remains of urban glory and Doric columns lay shattered in the Secaucus Meadows, destined to be pulverized and buried as "fill" and offered as a "prepared" site for commercial development.

For a while, a fragment of a classical figure was visible among marble shards in a setting of macabre surrealist vérité. The message was terribly clear. Tossed into that Secaucus graveyard were about twenty-five centuries of classical culture and the standards of style, elegance, and grandeur that it gave to the dreams and constructions of western man. That turned the Jersey wasteland into a pretty classy dump.

Ada Louise Huxtable
New York City
1966, 1996

PREFACE

It was a symbol of the power and the romance of our railroads. It was one of those rare architectural masterpieces that are able to touch man's soul. Built as a landmark it was a monumental gateway meant to last through centuries. Yet Pennsylvania Station stood for little more than fifty years.

Today it is inconceivable that a building of such grandeur, a building that bore witness to so much of the nation's history, could be wiped away so capriciously. But when the Pennsylvania Railroad decided to destroy its beautiful station there was nothing to protect it; there was no law to prevent the destruction of our architectural treasures. It was not until most of Pennsylvania Station lay shattered in the Meadowlands of New Jersey that the Landmarks Preservation Commission in New York was given legal authority to act on its decisions. The great station that held the private histories of so many Americans had become our sacrificial lamb. It seemed that its death was necessary to make us realize what could be lost.

Pennsylvania Station has been gone from us for over twenty years. Since its demise we have weighed more carefully the remnants of our past. We have fought harder for the buildings that have shared the city with us, and we have measured their value in the ways they have enriched our lives.

The grand and noble station died a sad, inglorious death. The time has come to offer a fitting epitaph from Thomas Wolfe's *You Can't Go Home Again:*

> Few buildings are vast enough to hold the sound of time, and . . . there was a superb fitness in the fact that the one which held it better than all others should be a railroad station.

Pennsylvania Station glows in the winter dusk in this noble view, made looking south from the sixteenth floor of a nearby office building in November 1949.

METRO-NORTH COMMUTER RAIL COMPANY

CHAPTER ONE

THE BEGINNING
OF THE END

In the early evening sunset during that summer of 1964, they looked like the remains of an ancient Roman temple toppled by an earthquake. The thirty Doric columns that once stood thirty-five-feet high lay broken and shattered in the meadow, their pink granite surfaces reflecting the sun's rays. Passengers on the train heading for the city could see the ruins and marvel at the incongruity; for the train was not, after all, traveling the Italian countryside en route to Rome. It was plying the Pennsylvania Railroad's main line, speeding across the New Jersey Meadowlands from Philadelphia to New York, and the columns were not a transplanted Roman ruin but the melancholy remains of the once majestic Pennsylvania Station.

Across the Hudson, beyond the Secaucus meadows, the din of jackhammers and wrecking balls, of crashing marble and shattering glass, silenced voices and tightened nerves. Dust from what was now unwanted debris hung thick in the air. Like a recalcitrant tenant resisting eviction, the dust would be the last to leave.

The destruction of Pennsylvania Station had begun almost a year before, on October 28, 1963. At precisely nine o'clock on that drizzly Monday morning, the demolition crew appeared at the Thirty-third Street entrance and began jabbing at the thick granite walls with jackhammers, exposing the original delicate pink beneath the sooty surface.

"Just another job," the crew foreman told *New York Times* reporters as he watched his men pierce deeper into the station's hide. Less than two hours later the first of the six stone eagles that guarded the entrance was coaxed from its aerie and lowered to the ground. The captive bird was surrounded by a group of officials wearing symbolic hard hats. They clustered about their trophy and smiled for photographers. Once the servants of the sun, symbols of immortality, the stone birds that had perched atop the station now squatted on a city street, penned in by sawhorses as their station came down around them.

In all there were twenty-two eagles crowning the station, each weighing fifty-seven hundred pounds, each given its form by the noted sculptor Adolph A. Weinman. It was fitting that Alexander Cassatt, the Pennsylvania Railroad president, had chosen the eagle to preside over his station. The great bird had been the insignia of the Byzantine emperors. It had represented the Caesars as they claimed the Roman Empire. Cassatt's railroad station,

Her career at its inglorious end, one of the stone maidens carved for the station by Adolph A. Weinman lies amid other debris in the New Jersey Meadowlands. It is 1966, and the train in the background is heading for the great station's squalid successor.

whose Doric columns were inspired by the colonnade Bernini designed to enclose Rome's Piazza di San Pietro, was conceived as a monumental gateway, one that would grant access to all America.

Born into the Philadelphia aristocracy, contemporary of the novelist Henry James and the sculptor Augustus Saint-Gaudens and of Stanford White and Charles McKim, whose architectural firm would build the station, Alexander Cassatt understood the value of symbols. His travels had taken him through the great railroad stations of Europe, and he wanted to give his country her own symbol of progress. It was also fitting that he should want the gateway he built to delight the soul; his sense and love of beauty grew from the close bond he shared with his sister, the impressionist painter Mary Cassatt. Norman Jaffe, one of several architects alarmed by the Pennsylvania Railroad's plan of destruction, recently recalled his reasons for trying to marshal support among New Yorkers to save Pennsylvania Station. "It reflected a civilization that had the patience, wealth, and faith in the future to build such a great space just for getting off a train," he said. "It was made of marble instead of Formica, and it was built to last for generations, not just for fifteen minutes."

By the summer of 1964 the men with jackhammers had penetrated the Seventh Avenue entrance and demolished the elegant arcade of shops, a miniature boulevard of bookstores, bonbonniéres, and haberdashers reminiscent of the famous arcades of Milan and Naples. For the traveler arriving from another part of the country, the Pennsylvania Station arcade was more than an avenue of stores; it was a metaphor proclaiming the city that lay outside the station's doors.

The wrecking crew had also broken the marble steps of the forty-foot-wide Grand Stairway, at whose summit one could stand beside the bronze statue of Cassatt and gaze in three directions to behold the vast temple of space and light. Descending the stairs, one entered the most awesome interior space in the city. Inspired by the baths of Caracalla, as well as those of Titus and Diocletian, and by the Basilica of Constantine, the main waiting room of Pennsylvania Station was comparable in size to the nave of Saint Peter's in Rome. Sometimes called the Great Room, this area was actually modeled after the Roman baths' tepidarium, or warm room, a central hall around which the other rooms of the baths were grouped. Like that of a tepidarium, the ceiling consisted of a series of barrel vaults with clerestory windows directly below, illuminating the space with natural light. This room, which extended two city blocks, north to south, from Thirty-third to Thirty-first streets, was constructed of travertine marble taken from quarries near Tivoli, Italy. It is said that this was the first time such marble was imported for use in an American building. Travertine is a warm, honey-colored stone from which most of the churches and palaces of ancient Rome were built. It was used to build Hadrian's tomb and the Roman Coliseum in the first century A.D. and the Basilica of Saint Peter's fifteen centuries later. The station's eight Corinthian columns, 7 feet in diameter and 60 feet high, carried the eye in a breathtaking sweep past the dusty Jules Guerin wall maps and lunette windows, toward a coffered octagonal ceiling 150 feet high. At the north and south ends of the room, colonnades of Ionic columns, 31 feet high, flanked the entrances.

In this room, where sunlight filtered down through soot-encrusted windows,

During the station's demolition, several of the Weinman eagles that once guarded its entrances await their fate as curiosities in shopping malls and suburban depots.

time stood still. A half century of emotion hung in the air, texturing it with memories of two world wars, a worldwide depression, and the private histories of people coming and going, meeting and parting. So many Americans passed through this room, leaving so much of themselves behind, that it seemed to belong to all of them, as Thomas Wolfe wrote in *You Can't Go Home Again*:

> For here, as nowhere else on earth, men were brought together for a moment at the beginning or end of their innumerable journeys, here one saw their greetings and farewells, here, in a single instant, one got the entire picture of the human destiny. Men came and went, they passed and vanished, and all were moving through the moments of their lives to death, all made small tickings in the sound of time—but the voice of time remained aloof and unperturbed, a drowsy and eternal murmur below the immense and distant roof.

Now, in the sticky heat of a New York July, less than a year since the demolition began, the waiting room looked like the bombed-out shell of a great cathedral. Coils and wires hung like entrails from its cracked and open walls. The men with jackhammers filled the air with noise and dust. The noise violated memory; the dust smelled of death.

The great station did not enter its final struggle unattended. Two years before, in the winter of 1962, when it was learned that the ailing Pennsylvania Railroad was attempting to save itself by sacrificing Penn Station, a group of architects gathered to protest. In the beginning there were six. Calling themselves the Action Group for Better Architecture in New York, or AGBANY, Norman Jaffe, Peter Samton, Jordan Gruzen, Diana Kirsch, and Elliot Willensky met in the Sixty-first Street brownstone of their chairman, Norval White, to consider ways to prevent the hungry Goliath from devouring its own creation. "We were so emotionally committed, and it was so much the right thing to do," Jaffe told me. "We thought we'd get all kinds of support. We felt that we were on the side of right and that right would win." But the six architects did not count on the indifference of New Yorkers toward their railroad station. Willensky, now a member of the Landmarks Preservation Commission and the official historian of Brooklyn, described the attitude they were up against: "I would say there was no consciousness among most New Yorkers of the value of old architecture. It wasn't so much a desire to wipe out the old. It was simply a lack of recognition of the old having any kind of wealth."

At one point AGBANY's lawyer discussed with Jaffe the possibility of arguing for preservation of Pennsylvania Station on the grounds that the building occupied what was once Thirty-second Street and that since public property had been given to the Pennsylvania Railroad for the accommodation of the public, the railroad had no legal right to sell it. But the City Planning Commission had no jurisdiction over the preservation of the city's architecture. The commission hearings, which were scheduled to be held in January 1963, would determine not whether the Pennsylvania Railroad had the right to tear down its station and sell the land but whether the Madison Square Garden Corporation should be given a zoning variance to build its new sports arena there.

As the months went by it became clear to the AGBANY founders and their supporters that being on the side of right did not guarantee success. Jaffe worked for the architect Philip Johnson at the time and remembered his prophetic advice about preserving old buildings. "You can picket all you want, but it's not going to do any good," Johnson told him. "If you want to save Pennsylvania Station, you have to buy it." At one point Norval White suggested just that. He wanted the Port of New York Authority (today called the Port Authority of New York and New Jersey) to buy Pennsylvania Station and administer it as it does other major gateways in the city. But by then the architects knew that they were whistling in the wind. "We didn't think we had much of a chance," White told me. "People never heard of landmarks in 1962. They didn't realize what they were about to lose."

Throughout the year letters in the *New York Times* protested the station's threatened demolition, but they were random shouts against the general silence of an apathetic public. In truth hardly anyone was listening.

Finally, on August 2, 1962, shortly past five in the afternoon, the six architects gathered in front of the station's Seventh Avenue entrance for a grand rally. With them were close to two hundred of their colleagues. Architects like Philip Johnson, Ulrich Franzen, Charles Evans Hughes, Jr., and John Johansen walked with writer Aline Saarinen, widow of the architect Eero Saarinen, who had designed the CBS building. The critic Lewis Mumford was there with the White House special consultant on the arts August Heckscher. They carried placards that read, DON'T DEMOLISH IT! POLISH IT! and SAVE YOUR GREAT STATION. One said simply, SHAME!

Some of the protesters had just come from a press conference the AGBANY architects had held across the street at the Statler Hotel. Fittingly the Statler (originally known as the Hotel Pennsylvania and today named the New York Penta) had been designed by McKim, Mead and White, the architectural firm that had designed Pennsylvania Station. It had been commissioned by the Pennsylvania Railroad five years after the station was completed to accommodate incoming passengers. The picketers walked in a double line beneath the stone eagles, occasionally breaking their mission's somber mood to greet one another.

They must have seemed an odd lot to the commuters who walked past them in the heat of an August afternoon. Men with rolled-up shirt sleeves suspiciously eyed the group, with their elegant suits and smart dresses, their artistically designed red-and-blue placards. In 1962 people picketed for better wages or shorter hours; they gathered at rallies to protest segregation and to ban the bomb. It was not a time when well-dressed professionals fought for art or principle.

And in 1962 people did not mind doing away with the old. "There was a feeling that the old was valueless," Kent Barwick, a former chairman of the Landmarks Preservation Commission, said. It seemed that there was still so much of the old around, and this dark, soot-covered building that served as nothing more than a place to board a train was surely expendable. "People wanted automobiles, suburban houses. There wasn't much affection for the city itself around the country."

So the commuters hardly saw the building whose life was on the line.

All they did see were these people in pin-striped suits with their educated voices and with their strange placards. They did not understand that something belonging to all of them would soon be destroyed.

"We had to cry out," Peter Samton, one of the six AGBANY architects, remembered. "We knew as we walked the picket line that we didn't have much of a chance. But we had to be there. Here was a major building . . . a city landmark . . . being torn down in a ruthless way without any protection. It was a violation . . . it was a rape of a portion of the city. We all felt we were being violated, and we had to scream out."

Ironically, just a few months before, on April 21, a City Landmarks Preservation Commission had been established by Mayor Robert Wagner and charged with "protecting structures and areas of historic or aesthetic importance." Concern over the loss of New York architecture had long been shared by the Municipal Art Society and by James Felt, the chairman of the City Planning Commission. In 1957 the Municipal Art Society had published a forty-page list of structures built in New York City before 1930 that the society felt were worthy of preservation. Trinity Church was on the list, along with the Plaza Hotel, the Dakota apartments, and the Brooklyn Bridge. McKim, Mead and White's Metropolitan Club was there with the Villard mansion (now the home of the Municipal Art Society) and, of course, Charles McKim's masterpiece, Pennsylvania Station. It was this list that would form the impetus for the emerging Landmarks Preservation Commission.

There was beginning to be a strong feeling about old buildings "brought about in many ways by Robert Moses and his urban renewal projects," Geoffrey Platt, the first chairman of the Landmarks Preservation Commission, recalled in an interview at his midtown architectural firm. "Moses had pushed his projects through in such an arrogant, high-handed manner. As a result, a great many neighborhoods were swept away.

"James Felt was the key man in making the Landmarks Preservation Commission come about," Platt said. (Platt was chairman of the zoning committee of the Municipal Art Society at the time.) "Felt made an address to the society, saying something should be done about preserving old buildings. Harmon Goldstone [president of the Municipal Art Society] and I had lunch with him. 'I'll help you with this,' Felt said. 'You, Harmon Goldstone, write a letter to the mayor recommending that [an advisory] committee be formed and I'll see that he gets it, and I'll see that he does something about it.' And he did."

In 1961 a thirteen-member advisory committee was appointed, and in 1962 it was formally constituted as a mayoral commission. But it would be another three years before a landmarks law would be passed, giving the Landmarks Preservation Commission authority to act on its decisions. By then the jackhammers had done most of their work, and Pennsylvania Station was just a year away from total destruction.

By autumn 1964 the concourse had already been gutted. This magnificent train shed of steel and glass, modeled after the great stations of Europe, had been a triumph of style and emotion. It was Charles McKim's intention to give the stranger entering the city something familiar, something to soften the anxiety of first encounter. A train shed that recalled the Gare Montparnasse and the Gare du Nord in Paris and the stations in Frankfurt and Dresden would provide a visual and emotional link to other major cities of the world. It would also provide America with a monumental gateway, an entrance to one of its great metropolitan cities. The concourse was a success in accomplishing its every intention. It was a wonder of detail, from the sweeping steel barrel arches that curved across the glass roof to the iron candelabra that hung in the vast space and down again to the train gates, with their cupola tops and Roman corner columns.

Until the early thirties, when the concourse floor was extended to the west over the track area, passengers could look below at the trains arriving and departing and above to the latticed steel arches etched against the sky, rising one hundred feet at their apex. In constructing the concourse roof McKim wanted to maintain the simplicity of design that was thematic of the station and, at the same time, to provide a visual transition between the monumental main waiting room and the utilitarian yards and tracks. To accomplish this and to avoid monotony of design, the engineering firm of Westinghouse, Church, Kerr & Co. was called upon to construct a series of intersecting barrel arches of varying widths and sizes, all within a space prescribed by the columns, arches, and domes of the concourse itself. This difficult piece of roofing required more steel than would have been used had McKim been satisfied with a simpler design. But to Cassatt and McKim, the visual integrity of this room outweighed its great cost.

On October 29, 1964, as the station's innards were still being pulled away, a crane especially designed for working in cramped quarters pushed its way into the concourse and lowered a five-ton steel grillage into a six-foot hole next to track 19. Soon the new Madison Square Garden sports arena would begin to rise like an awkward phoenix from Pennsylvania Station's ashes. As with the lowering of the stone eagles on an October morning the year before, the occasion was marked by ceremony.

The Bethlehem Steel Company had located Stanley Jesse Willet, a seventy-seven-year-old retired ironworker who had helped build the second Madison Square Garden thirty-nine years before, when it was located on Eighth Avenue between Forty-ninth and Fiftieth streets. Bethlehem press agents posed Mr. Willet with a hard hat in his hand, signaling to the crane operator to begin work. There would be 206 more grillages inserted into holes in the station's floor, so that the Garden's steel framework could be fastened to them.

The skeletal frame of Pennsylvania Station would remain standing as the new Madison Square Garden was born within it. The combined work of construction and destruction was complicated because it had to be done in three overlapping phases. The original station had to be torn down, the new Madison Square Garden sports arena and office building had to be constructed, and a new Pennsylvania Station put together—all this while trains continued to run beneath the surface.

Dust and debris were the constant companions of passengers who used the station during this time. Jackhammers assaulted their ears as they tried to unlearn familiar routes and find new ways to reach their trains. The disorientation was annoying but superficial. The subtler feelings of loss would come later.

Overleaf: Two 1964 photographs document the last days of the main waiting room. The structural-steel columns rising from the rubble-strewn floor in the picture at the right will help support the new Madison Square Garden.

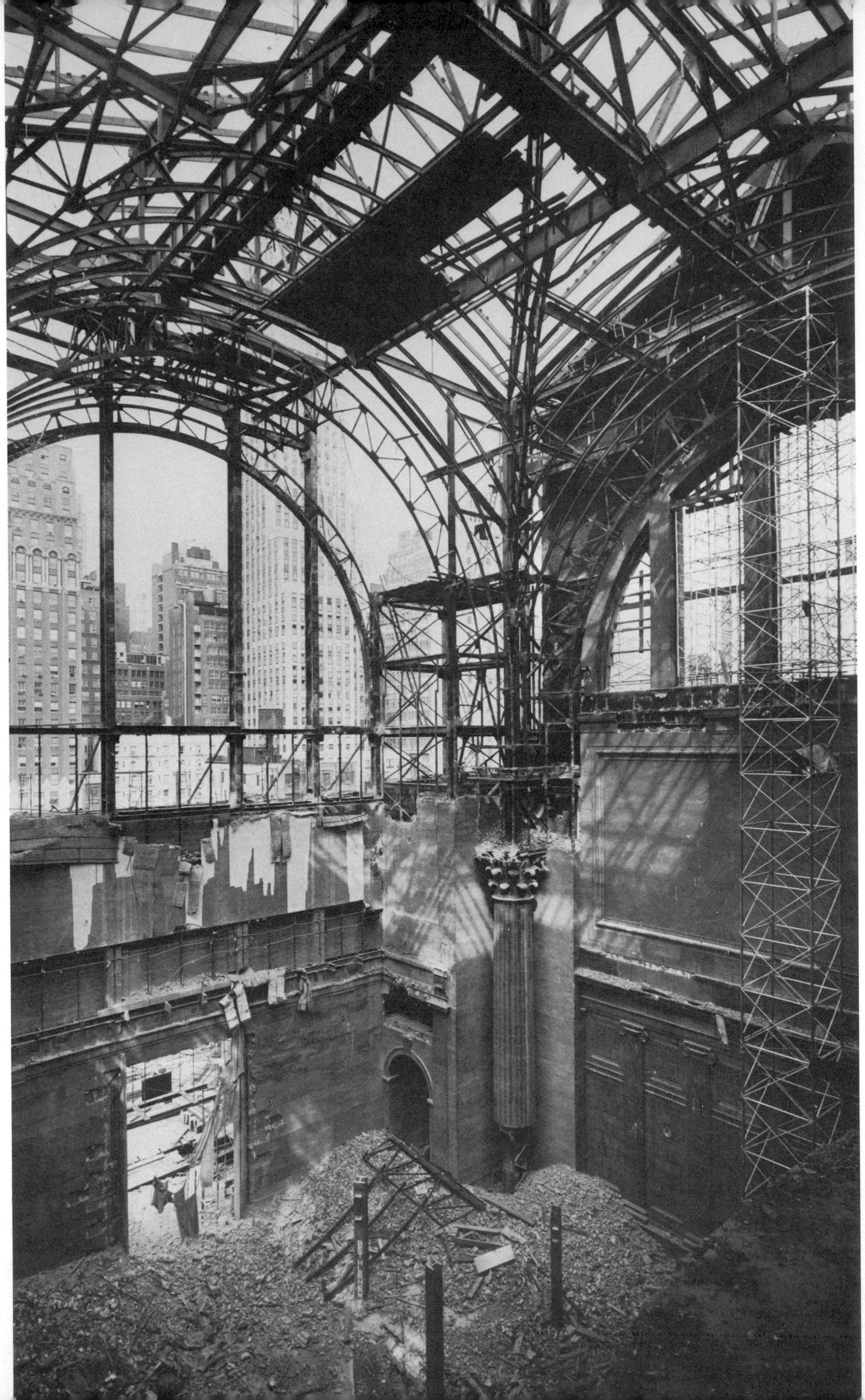

NORMAN McGRATH

"Great indoor spaces ennoble people," said Norman Jaffe. "They give people a sense of worth. They make us pause and wonder, 'Oh, isn't it remarkable, this space. It's indoors, it's high, it's vast, and man built it; therefore, man must do something noble.'" It was not simply architecture that the AGBANY architects were trying to defend, it was the human spirit.

But what excited most people in 1964 was the new, and this ultramodern sports complex that the Madison Square Garden Corporation was going to erect was not only new, it was something many New Yorkers felt they should have. The corporation understood this. Before a decision was made to tear down Pennsylvania Station they invested hundreds of thousands of dollars in architectural fees and engineering surveys. By the fall of 1962, before they had even obtained a zoning variance to build a 22,000-seat sports arena on a site zoned for no more than 2,500 seats, they already had commitments for $130 million in building rentals for their two proposed office towers.

In an effort to please the public and save a landmark, Norman Jaffe suggested that the twin office towers be built over the top of Pennsylvania Station, above the Seventh Avenue entrance where the carriage drives were located. According to his design, the sports arena would be built two blocks west, over the Pennsylvania's rail yards. But that would put the sports complex at a distance from the trains and the subways, something the Madison Square Garden Corporation was opposed to. Besides, since they were getting such strong support for their own design, why bother to accommodate a handful of architects.

Even the Pennsylvania Railroad was anxious to be rid of Pennsylvania Station. For ten years the financially strapped line had been trying to divest itself of the structure, all the while allowing it to fall into disrepair. The glass-domed roof in the concourse was darkened, grimy with soot. Broken windows were replaced with sheets of metal. "They didn't take good care of it," said Archie Harris, a former baggageman for the old station. "It was dangerous when it would rain because the rain came in from the broken glass panes." In the main waiting room the six lunette windows were clouded with dirt, and the Jules Guerin murals beneath them were little more than dark, colorless expanses. Outside, the pink granite had turned a dull city gray. During those ten years the station sat in shabby splendor, desecrated by indifference and the railroad's desperate attempts to remain solvent.

In 1958 a huge plastic clamshell glowing with fluorescent light and housing electronically controlled ticket booths was installed in the main waiting room, its wire tentacles digging into the Corinthian columns for support. "They were able to eliminate over a thousand jobs with that clamshell," Harris said. As out of place in McKim's Great Room as a hot dog stand in the Louvre, the clamshell was only one of many violations perpetrated against the station's aesthetics. Shiny late-model cars revolved on platforms in the arcade and main waiting room, as visually intrusive as the garish advertisements in glass boxes that were attached to the travertine walls. Near the Thirty-third Street entrance to the main waiting room a series of stores with modern glass fronts was installed, intruding on its subdued elegance. The effect caused Lewis Mumford to observe in his book *The Highway and the City*, "A West Forty-second Street garishness and

The steel framework for the new Pennsylvania Station's concrete ceiling bisects the vast main waiting room; the canvas screen beyond walls off the arcade.

tawdriness characterize the whole reconstruction." Because the new ticket booths took up the space formerly occupied by the telegraph offices, a Western Union booth had to be built on the east side of the waiting room, at the foot of the steps to the arcade. If these modifications were intended to boost revenues and make Pennsylvania Station economically viable, they were, in the end, as useless as they were ugly.

Three years after the installation of the new ticket booth, in July 1961, the Madison Square Garden Corporation was formed. Just over a year

By late 1966 the old station had entirely vanished and Madison Square Garden occupied the site of its steel-and-glass concourse.

later, on September 23, 1962, an architectural rendering of the proposed Madison Square Garden Center appeared in the *New York Times* under the headline BATTLE OVER FUTURE OF PENN STATION CONTINUES. But it was clear that the battle was lost.

Norman Jaffe watched sadly as the inevitable happened. Looking back at that period of twenty years ago, he said, "Here was the City of New York taking one of its great assets and swapping it for more tax revenue, or whatever else they felt was going to be an immediate asset, rather than

27

thinking of the city's long-term well-being. It led me to believe that New York was not a city, not a place that one could look to for a sense of the past, but a commercial phenomenon that was characterized by a 'Here today, gone tomorrow' attitude. . . . Unpack your pushcart, make a deal, and get out."

Irving Felt, the president of the Madison Square Garden Corporation, defended destruction with arguments that echoed Jaffe's observations. Felt spoke of the $120 million that would be pumped into the construction industry and the estimated $5 million in new tax revenue to the city.

In August 1962, as the fight to save the station intensified, *Time* magazine quoted Philip Johnson as saying, "You realize that man can build nobly." The same article gave Felt's reply: "Fifty years from now, when it's time for our Center to be torn down, there will be a new group of architects who will protest."

Ironically, James Felt, the chairman of the City Planning Commission, a man who had been troubled by the increasing loss of old and valuable buildings and who had encouraged the formation of the Landmarks Preservation Commission, disqualified himself from the Madison Square Garden zoning hearings because his brother Irving was president of the Madison Square Garden Corporation.

By January 1966 a concrete slab had been poured across the concourse floor. It would act as the ceiling of the new Pennsylvania Station, and the famous one-hundred-foot-high steel-and-glass skylight roof would be brought down and destroyed. That month the first of forty-eight columns that would form the perimeter of the circular sports arena was brought in and hoisted into place. Again the occasion was turned into ceremony: Irving Felt pretended to bolt a column into place with a gold-plated wrench.

Another summer came, the final one for the old station. In July 1966 the last of the statuary that stood atop the building was lowered. The four sets of stone women, representing day and night, who embraced the enormous clocks above each of the entrances were hoisted into the air and brought down. Jackhammers were still pushing into the stone columns close to the entrance. There were fifty men with jackhammers, working through the summer heat, hoping to level the entrance wall along Seventh Avenue by month's end.

By winter newspaper reports turned from destruction to progress. Gone were the melancholy pictures of Penn Station's ruins. Artists' renderings of the futuristic Madison Square Garden sports complex and the new streamlined Pennsylvania Station took their place. There was no more mention of travertine marble and pink Milford granite. Now people read about the concrete panels studded with pebbles that would be part of the edifice of the new sports arena. The panels did not come from quarries in Tivoli but from the Plasticrete Corporation, in Hamden, Connecticut. In the new Pennsylvania Station red metal doors replaced the elegant iron folding gates that led to the tracks. Iron candelabra that once hung in the great glass train shed would not fit the new fifteen-foot ceilings pressing down on travelers. Fluorescent tubes would do.

The eagles found homes in parks and suburban train stations. Four of them went to Philadelphia, where they sit atop a bridge near the Pennsylvania

Railroad's Thirtieth Street Station. Two were placed in front of the new Pennsylvania Station, looking as alien as emperors guarding a poorhouse. The bronze statue of Alexander Cassatt was adopted by Cassatt's alma mater, Rensselaer Polytechnic Institute, in Troy, New York. A statue of his successor, Samuel Rea, stands in shadow before the entrance to 2 Pennsylvania Plaza.

Adolph Weinman's eight stone maidens, who had graced the four entrances, did not fare as well: there was little use for the twelve-foot art nouveau goddesses. The Brooklyn Museum took one of the women representing night. Ringwood Manor in New Jersey has two—which have been cut in half and left in a parking lot. The remaining statues were thrown in with the rest of the station, the tons of Tivoli marble and Milford granite carted to the New Jersey Meadowlands.

There had been talk of preserving eighteen of the Doric columns that had surrounded the station. These could be used to create a colonnade at Battery Park, with one of the eagles presiding over the columns. But the trip downtown proved too costly, so these, too, joined the others on the rubble heap at Secaucus.

"There's a funny cycle that occurs in the history of a building," Kent Barwick, former chairman of the Landmarks Preservation Commission, said recently. "It is very much appreciated when it is put up, then it sort of disappears into the city when other buildings become more noticeable or celebrated. And just a little while before it is rediscovered, it is thought to be absolutely worthless. That's the dangerous moment for a building. If Pennsylvania Station was given five more years—maybe three more years, a little more time—Penn Station would have been here and alive today. Look at Radio City Music Hall."

If timing played a part in the station's demise, it also had a lot to do with its birth. It was timing that had enabled Alexander Cassatt to build the station he had been dreaming about for years. If it had been simply a case of putting marble to mortar, of finding the right architect to express Cassatt's intentions, Pennsylvania Station would have been built long before Cassatt became president of the railroad. But in order to build the station the Pennsylvania's tracks and trains had to be able to get to it. Between the country's premier railroad and its star city flowed a river. As in the riddle of an ancient fairy tale adapted for a new century, the man who found the means to cross the river would be the man to build the new railroad station. And as in a fairy tale, fate interceded at just the right moment to make one man's dreams come true.

CHAPTER TWO

A VISION EMERGES

On a sunny day in late June 1901, Charles McKim gathered with several friends to walk through the ancient streets and amble into the halls and the basilicas of one of his favorite cities. To McKim, Rome embodied the spirit of man expressed in architecture. He so loved the Eternal City that he had been the impetus behind the American Academy in Rome, where students of architecture would come not just to apprentice but to develop their sense of beauty by meditating among the monuments. For McKim these ageless buildings were poems set in stone, representing the perfect marriage of intellect and imagination.

By late afternooon the group had arrived at the Baths of Caracalla. Sprawling across thirty-three acres, the famous baths had been a gathering place where Romans attended to business and took their pleasure while bathing in mountain waters that flowed through aqueducts into a complex of cold, hot, and steam baths. Wrestlers, boxers, and runners worked out in the baths' halls. Poets, philosophers, and statesmen expounded to all who would listen in areas reserved for public oratory. Romans had reason to love their baths; not only were they a triumph of engineering, they were magnificent temples of space and light, built for the express purpose of pleasing the citizenry.

Approaching the baths on that summer day, McKim was so struck by their beauty that although he had at the time no commission to design a building patterned after them, he not only set to drawing the massive baths but to hiring some nearby workmen to pose among them in order to give scale and movement to his sketches.

In the summer of 1901, Alexander Cassatt was in Europe as well, on one of his frequent holidays abroad. On another summer's day eighteen years before, Cassatt had come upon the ruins of the Baths of Caracalla and, like McKim, had been impressed by their beauty. This summer he was in Paris, visiting his sister, Mary. The sixty-two-year-old Cassatt had emerged just two years before from a self-imposed retirement to take over the presidency of the Pennsylvania Railroad after the sudden death of Frank Thomson, its sixth president.

In 1882, at the young age of forty-two, Cassatt had resigned his job as first vice president of the railroad. His decision perplexed rival railroad titans and exasperated the officers of the Pennsylvania Railroad. What had come

The architect Charles Follen McKim found his inspiration for Pennsylvania Station's main waiting room from the tepidarium of the Baths of Caracalla.

Alexander Cassatt (left), president of the Pennsylvania Railroad, wanted a truly monumental station. Charles McKim (right), head of the preeminent turn-of-the-century architectural firm McKim, Mead and White, gave him one.

over a man in the prime of his life to put aside a brilliant career working for a railroad that he cared about so intensely? At first it was thought that his having been passed over for the presidency in 1880 in favor of George P. Roberts had depressed and angered him. But as time went by it became clear that Cassatt really wanted to put aside the pressures of his railroad duties, no matter how devoted he was to the company, and simply enjoy himself.

For the next seventeen years, Alexander Cassatt did just that. Born to wealth, he thoroughly enjoyed the pleasures of a leisured life, which included furnishing four elegant houses and taking frequent European trips. With time at his disposal, he spent great stretches of it abroad with his family, visiting his favorite cities and exploring the far reaches of the world. There was time to sit for a portrait by his sister or simply to pass long afternoons in her company. At home he devoted much energy to his lifelong passion, the breeding and racing of horses.

He was a complex man who enjoyed power immensely and had never been reluctant to use it for the good of his railroad. But he had another side as well, a gentle counterpoint to his drive and ambition. As a prospective groom he had spent days traveling between Philadelphia and Altoona, Pennsylvania, where the couple would reside, to inspect bolts of wallpaper for the new home he would share with his bride. "I had to send back the paper we selected on Saturday," he told his bride to be. "I found that the blue rubbed off so easily that your dresses would have been spoiled." He became unusually involved in details of the wedding plans, subjecting everything to inspection, including the bridesmaids' gowns.

Cassatt doted on his wife. Throughout his life he seemed most comfortable when she was not far from his side. Lois Cassatt did not get along with her famous sister-in-law, Mary, with whom Alexander shared a close relationship. The two women saw each other in a mutually unflattering light.

Mary thought Lois too concerned with social ambition, and Lois, making no allowance for artistic temperament, considered Mary too self-absorbed. It was also difficult for Lois, a woman of strict religious upbringing, to share her husband's passion for horseracing, a passion that Cassatt's parents and sisters, Mary and Lydia, also embraced.

His retirement from the railroad gave Cassatt the opportunity to enjoy Chesterbrook, a farm he had purchased in 1881 on the outskirts of Philadelphia where he bred the horses he bought from all over the world. Eventually, Chesterbrook would spread over six hundred acres, accommodating the animals Cassatt entered in every major race in the country. He became well-known as a breeder, and some of his thoroughbreds earned very good purses. After his taste for racing dulled, Cassatt turned Chesterbrook into a breeding farm for hackneys, crossbreeding the English horse with the American trotter.

In the early 1890s the Cassatts spent much of their time abroad. With their children in boarding schools or off on their own, Cassatt and his wife had more time on their hands. Sailing had begun to interest him, and he chartered yachts for trips within the United States and abroad. In 1895 he bought *Star of the Sea*, an elaborately fitted vessel for which he paid over $500,000, and rechristened it *Enterprise*. With his new yacht and his horse farm, Alexander Cassatt was quite content to spend the rest of his life traveling with his family, showing his horses, and living a life of parties and social functions suitable to a country squire. Although he still maintained a seat on the Pennsylvania's board of directors, he showed no desire to return to railroading full time.

On January 30, 1897, George P. Roberts, the man whose election to the presidency of the Pennsylvania Railroad in 1882 was thought by some to have prompted Cassatt's early retirement, died of heart failure. The railroad, in a major slump, required a bold visionary to succeed Roberts. In 1893 a depression had swept the country. Brought on in part by rate wars among the nation's railroads, battles that were undermining the solvency of the country's entire railroad system, the depression eroded the Pennsylvania's profits. It was during this time that Roberts unwisely inaugurated major improvements along the company's track systems without securing additional capital to finance his program.

Alexander Cassatt deliberated with the rest of the board of directors as a successor was chosen. If Cassatt harbored any thought that he would be that man, there is no evidence of it. At the time of the board meeting, he was making preparations to take *Enterprise* on a lengthy cruise, and the railroad elected Cassatt's good friend, Frank Thomson, as Robert's successor. A company man with little imagination, Thomson was seemingly ill-equipped to turn the troubled railroad around. Cassatt may have had misgivings about Thomson's running the railroad, but he never expressed them. The election over, Cassatt went back to the business of preparing for another holiday.

Frank Thomson bore the burden of running the Pennsylvania for two short years. He died on June 5, 1899, aged fifty-eight. Four days later, on June 9, the board of directors offered the presidency to Alexander Cassatt.

He was reluctant to assume the job. He knew, as did all the members of the board, that he was the person most qualified to run the railroad, and he cared enough about the Pennsy to want to see it healthy again. But the physical cost to him might well prove enormous. Roberts had died of heart failure, and Thomson had not reached sixty before his heart gave out. In spite of Cassatt's leisured life he was not a healthy man. At the age of fifty-five he had suffered a heart attack, and now, at sixty, he was naturally reluctant to risk what might cut short the life he so enjoyed. Nevertheless, weighing the physical demands of the job and the fact that he would have to put aside his horses and his pleasure cruises, Cassatt finally decided to accept the presidency.

If Cassatt had reservations about his decision, they were not shared by members of his board of directors nor by industrial and railroad magnates throughout the country, all of whom breathed a collective sigh of relief when, finally, a man of talent had taken over the railroad. Despite his apprehension, reentry into railroading must have been a heady experience for Cassatt. By the turn of the century, in spite of its setbacks, the Pennsylvania was the largest, wealthiest, and busiest road in the country. Its reputation as the "Standard Railroad of the World" had been made years before, and Cassatt knew as well as anyone who had elected him that he was the man to bring his company full throttle into the twentieth century.

Yet, an obstacle stood between Cassatt and one of his great ambitions. The Hudson River, which gave Manhattan the famous harbor that made New York an international port, kept the Pennsylvania Railroad from the city shores. For thirty years Alexander Cassatt had sought a way to get the Pennsylvania trains into Manhattan, but the river refused to be conquered by bridge or tunnel. A bridge, often proposed, would have required a span twice that of the Brooklyn Bridge and would have carried a price tag of more than fifty million dollars. Tunnels under the Hudson were hardly an alternative, since steam locomotives would likely asphyxiate passengers and crew before delivering them from one side of the river to the other. The stubborn, mile-wide body of water separated one of the most powerful railroads from the nation's premier city; and if there was one thing Cassatt wanted to accomplish during his presidency, it was to see the Pennsylvania's trains enter New York City.

In 1891, while in retirement, Cassatt had persuaded George Roberts to investigate the feasibility of a tunnel between Staten Island and Long Island through which the railroad could extend its tracks along a southerly course from New Jersey. Once on Long Island, the tracks would fork: one section would enter Manhattan over an East River bridge while the second section would continue north, connecting with the New York, New Haven and Hartford Railroad. If Cassatt's plan worked, not only would the Pennsylvania run its trains into New York City, it would have a means to reach into New England—all the while circumventing the obstinate Hudson. An engineering study undertaken by the railroad proved Cassatt's plan feasible, but instead of simplifying the problem it left George Roberts with yet another avenue to investigate. Should the Pennsylvania Railroad spend its resources trying to build a Hudson River bridge, a Hudson River tunnel, or should it pursue Cassatt's bridge and tunnel idea? Each avenue had its own formidable obstacles, any one of which could present a dead end.

It was at this point, in the summer of 1892, that Roberts sent Samuel Rea, his vice president, to England to investigate the South London Railway, which was trying electric power in its subway system. Two years earlier,

in 1890, while speaking before the Congressional Committee on Commerce, Rea had summed up his feelings about tunnels: "They are expensive to maintain and disagreeable to the passengers, who would probably prefer crossing on ferries to trusting themselves on slow trains running through damp and chilly submarine tunnels." On his return from London in 1893, he remained unconvinced that a tunnel was practical for the Pennsylvania Railroad. Although impressed with the new electric locomotives that were pulling London's trains beneath its streets, he did not feel that electric traction would work in America, where locomotives had to handle much heavier tonnages.

By 1901, however, Rea had changed his mind. The Baltimore and Ohio's successful five-year operation of electric trains made it clear to him that tunneling not only was feasible but was the only way for the Pennsylvania Railroad to enter New York City. Rea, now Alexander Cassatt's fourth vice president, was anxious to persuade his chief to accept his idea.

The Pennsylvania Railroad Station at Exchange Place, in Jersey City (shown here in an engraving from around 1890), marked the end of the line for passengers heading into New York. Here they had to board the ferries that would carry them across to Manhattan. It was an interruption that infuriated Cassatt.

35

A cable from Rea reached Cassatt in Paris. It urged him to attend the opening ceremonies of the Gare du Quai d'Orsay, an event that would be watched by all of Europe. Rising on the banks of the Seine, the magnificent beaux-arts building stood proudly in the company of the Eiffel Tower and the Arc de Triomphe. But it was not the building that Rea wanted Cassatt to see. Inside, under a concourse of steel and glass, history was being made. The Gare du Quai d'Orsay, an extension of the Orléans railway, was the first electrified railroad terminal, the real-life prototype of Cassatt's dream. Into it ran trains powered solely by electricity. They came through tunnels running along the Seine and under the streets of Paris, tunnels massively walled against the river. Here Cassatt saw the means by which the Hudson could be conquered.

In September 1901 Cassatt returned to his offices on Broad Street in Philadelphia to consult with his chief engineer and to set his plans in motion. Three months later, on December 12, he announced to the nation that the Pennsylvania Railroad would build a series of tunnels beneath the Hudson River so that his railroad's trains could enter New York City. On that day Cassatt also announced the planned construction of a magnificent station, a monumental gateway to a great metropolis.

On April 24, 1902, just ten months after his visit to Rome and barely four months after Cassatt's announcement, Charles McKim wrote a letter to his friend and collaborator the American sculptor Augustus Saint-Gaudens: "I reached Washington on Sunday night and left yesterday . . . afternoon, in response to a despatch from President Cassatt, asking me to meet him this morning in Philadelphia, in relation to a new terminal depot of the Pennsylvania Railroad to be built in New York, and which, as you will be glad to hear, was placed under our direction."

Serendipity decreed that these men, who had been so impressed by the Roman baths they had viewed eighteen years apart from each another, would now find themselves sharing those separate impressions to build the Pennsylvania Railroad's station. It was as though each had discovered half of a treasure map and had to wait for a fateful meeting to put the pieces together. But that is where happenstance ended, for it was fitting and inevitable that Cassatt would call upon Charles McKim to help design his station.

By the turn of the century the architectural firm of McKim, Mead and White had made its imprint on New York City. From their offices in a narrow cast-iron building on lower Broadway, this improbable trio produced some of the most outstanding buildings the city had yet seen. The firm, barely twenty years old, had responded elegantly to the lament of Edith Wharton, who, in her biography, described the New York of the 1870s as a "cramped horizontal gridiron of a town without towers, porticoes, fountains, or perspectives, hidebound in its deadly uniformity of mean ugliness."

By the beginning of the twentieth century, one could not travel far in Manhattan without coming upon a tower or a portico designed by the firm, from Stanford White's extravagantly ornate Madison Square Garden, at Madison Square between Twenty-sixth and Twenty-seventh streets, crowned by Augustus Saint-Gaudens's controversial statue of a nude Diana, to the stately splendor of Charles McKim's Low Memorial Library, at Columbia

Stanford White used yellow brick and terra-cotta to enliven further the facade of his exuberant Madison Square Garden. Atop the three-hundred-foot tower, which was patterned on the Giralda, in Seville, Augustus Saint-Gaudens's famous bronze Diana pivoted with the changing winds.

University. The Metropolitan, the Century, and the University clubs all were designed by McKim, Mead and White. Washington Arch, the Tiffany residence, and the Herald Building were theirs as well as several more buildings at Columbia, including the Avery Building, and, later, J. P. Morgan's private library. Their work also included Sherry's Hotel, on Fifth Avenue; and several blocks north, on Sixty-ninth Street, Stanford White redesigned William Whitney's elegant town house. For Henry Villard they created a palazzo-style grouping of brownstones on Madison Avenue and Fiftieth Street.

It was the town houses and country homes designed for the new, untaxed wealthy, the railroad barons and real estate magnates, that became the signature of the firm. McKim, Mead and White's ability to bring the richness of the Renaissance across the Atlantic and adapt it to American tastes made them instantly popular. By the turn of the century the firm had received over five hundred commissions, and two of the partners, Stanford White and Charles McKim, had become as familiar to society as Tiffany, Auchincloss, and Vanderbilt.

The three partners were different from one another, temperamentally and artistically. Stanford White, with his flaming red hair and commanding presence, was a self-propelled whirlwind. He was gregarious, impulsive, impatient, with little regard for formula. According to Charles C. Baldwin, the architect's biographer, "Lawrence Grant White tells of a draughtsman who came to his father in despair, saying that the axis of a scheme—as indicated—could not be maintained. 'Then,' said White, 'bend the axis.' "

Charles McKim, on the other hand, was a scholar, insisting always on historic truth. He was known to send young apprentices into the company's library to pore over drawings and documents not so much to copy the past as to use it. In fact, the finished product often looked entirely different from its inspiration. If White worked in a fury of inspiration, McKim plodded patiently.

White stretched his talents beyond architecture to designing jewelry, picture frames, and magazine covers. His buildings, with their emphasis on color and texture, beckoned you to enter, while McKim's buildings, with their pure classic lines spare of ornamentation, demanded more distant respect.

William Rutherford Mead, who had collaborated with McKim for six years before the firm of McKim, Mead and White was formed, was the most business-minded member of the firm. Lawrence Grant White has said it was Mead's "sound judgement, often lacking in the makeup of the other two men, which steered them safely through the shoals, and enabled them to weather the storms." McKim and White depended on Mead for ballast as each sailed off on his own way. Augustus Saint-Gaudens, a close friend of all three partners, once drew an amusing caricature of Mead holding onto two airborne kites, each flying off in the opposite direction. One kite bore White's name, the other McKim's. In addition to keeping the firm on course, Mead's sense of scale and proportion and his grasp of architectural planning were, according to Lawrence White, invaluable assets.

In December 1901, while Cassatt was announcing his tunnel plans to the world, Charles McKim was in the midst of a project to modernize the White House. The idea of enlarging an architecturally perfect building appalled most architects, including Charles McKim. When the possibility of moving the White House to a better location came up, McKim's reaction revealed how deeply he felt about the historic building. "Let me take it down stone by stone," he said, "and rebuild it."

The man who carried with him the memory of a summer's afternoon in Rome could no more alter a thing of beauty than destroy it. As for his own work, it had a noble simplicity, a quiet dignity with roots firmly planted in the monuments of the past. Lawrence White said of him, "Each building McKim produced was an architectural event." If Cassatt wanted a building that would conjure up trumpets rather than flutes and violins, he had found his architect.

Long before Cassatt wrote to Charles McKim, before word of Cassatt's plans to bring his railroad into New York reached the newspapers, the Pennsylvania Railroad hired Stuyvesant Real Estate Company to buy up secretly much of the land the railroad needed for its new station. It had been decided long before that the perfect place for the railroad terminal would be in an area on the West Side of Manhattan, just below Thirty-fourth Street and just a few blocks east of the Hudson River. While Stuyvesant was buying up blocks of Manhattan, across the river more agents working for the railroad were purchasing land on the edge of New Jersey.

The impact of what Cassatt saw in Paris must have resounded in his head as he and his wife boarded the White Star Lines *Celtic* that autumn for the trip home. It must have echoed impatiently when the ship docked in New York harbor on the first weekend in September and, once again, Cassatt had to wait as his luggage was placed, piece by piece, on a carriage. Then the bumpy ride down the West Side of Manhattan, past the warehouses and freight terminals of the New York Central Railroad. Finally, the ferry ride across the Hudson where all of this began. What must it have been like to look down at a river that had welcomed ships from all over the world but had refused his railroad entry, to look down at it and know that before long it would be conquered?

CHAPTER THREE

THE RIVER CROSSING

Hᴉs wife's dark blue brougham met Archer at the ferry and conveyed him luxuriously to the Pennsylvania terminus in Jersey City," wrote Edith Wharton in *The Age of Innocence*. "It was a somber snowy afternoon, and the gas-lamps were lit in the big reverberating station. As he paced the platform, waiting for the Washington express, he remembered that there were people who thought there would one day be a tunnel under the Hudson through which the trains of the Pennsylvania railway would run straight into New York. . . . The clanging and groaning of the train came nearer, and it staggered slowly into the station like a pre-laden monster into its lair. . . . Meanwhile the carriage had worked its way out of the coil about the station, and they were crawling down the slippery incline to the wharf, menaced by swaying coal carts, bewildered horses, disheveled express wagons, and an empty hearse."

It was here at Exchange Place, in Jersey City, on the western edge of the Hudson River, that the Pennsylvania Railroad trains came to a halt. They came from Philadelphia, Washington, and as far west as Chicago. Together with other roads, they brought passengers from as far south as Florida. Vacationers, tanned and rested from wintering in Palm Beach, would leave their well-appointed Pullman cars and stand alongside office clerks commuting to the city as they all waited for the ferries to dock.

The ferry terminal Edith Wharton described was a constant source of anxiety, since the Pennsylvania trains came into Jersey City and the terminal on street level, endangering the lives of people and horses who had to negotiate the grade crossings. This cavernous wooden structure served the railroad for sixteen years before a fire burned it to the ground.

The new ferry terminal, built in 1891, was of a dramatically modern design, with a steel-and-glass train shed whose arched roof, said to be the largest of its kind in the world, became a familiar beacon to approaching ferry boats. The waiting room was elevated in the new building, as were the tracks entering the terminal, so that passengers went directly from the waiting room to the upper-deck saloons on the ferries. This improvement eliminated encounters with the swaying coal carts and express wagons that had menaced Edith Wharton's hero. Oddly the Pennsylvania Railroad's proposal to raise its tracks above the city streets encountered fierce opposition

Manhattan's bustling, traffic-choked West Street added to the discomfort and inconvenience that attended the Pennsylvania Railroad passenger's progress into New York City. This picture, taken on a typically busy day in 1898, shows the Pennsylvania's terminal at the far left.

from Jersey City fathers. While the dispute was raging, several people were killed at the very grade crossings the railroad was trying to eliminate.

Another fire, in January 1898, brought this new terminal down, only to have a better one rise from its ashes. The train shed was built closer to the river, and the waiting room in the terminal was removed from the main area. Now passengers could move directly from their trains to the waiting ferries without adding to the congestion caused by those who had reason to linger in the terminal.

But none of these improvements could dispel the awkwardness and discomfort of the journey ahead. For as pleasant as the train ride might have been and as trouble-free as the transfer from train to boat might have become, the trip across the river was, to a great extent, at the mercy of uncontrollable forces. Dense fog would sometimes roll across the river, stealing visibility. Rain, wind, and sleet would whip the wooden boats, heaving them about in the turbulent waters. At times like this a pleasant fifteen-minute crossing could become an hour-long journey across the Styx. Alexander Cassatt's biographer, Patricia T. Davis, quotes George B. Roberts, a grandson of the man who was the Pennsylvania's president in the 1890s, as he described one of his boyhood ferry crossings:

> Everybody got out of cars and climbed the dark, iron stairs to the open deck, where there were benches in the sun and a fresh breeze from the harbor. Mother promised us a view of the Statue of Liberty and the Brooklyn Bridge and we began to climb on the life rafts and railings. . . . At last the boat was loaded, a bell rang in the wheelhouse and the engines began to vibrate. Then, like a sick elephant, the most appalling blast came from the ship's whistle . . . we spent the rest of the voyage under the dim gas lamps of our drawing room . . . mother with cold compresses of cologne, a bottle of Poland water and a box of Petit Beurre bisquits.

By 1892 several new ferry boats had been commissioned, including the *Cincinnati*, with its improved steering apparatus and with electric lights that replaced the noisome gas lamps. But on a cold, windswept day, when the Hudson churned and heaved, no amount of improved steering could suppress a passenger's prayers for safe delivery free from *mal de mer* to the shores of Manhattan.

Once arrived on that shore—at one of the Pennsylvania Railroad's three Manhattan ferry terminals (at Battery Place, Morris Street, and Cortlandt and Desbrosses streets) or the fourth one, in Brooklyn—passengers may have wondered why they had put themselves through the journey across the river or why they had even boarded a train in the first place. The west side of lower Manhattan, where the ferry depots of various railroads lined the shore, was a nightmare of carriages, wagons, and horse teams that passengers laden with suitcases tried to dodge as they searched for transportation to the heart of the city. The Pennsylvania's three Manhattan depots all bordered West Street, a cluttered strip of shoreline that was shared by warehouses and all the freight-handling facilities of the New York Central as well as those of other railroads. As it had on the Jersey side, the Pennsylvania Railroad ran into the usual bureaucratic resistance when it petitioned for a pedestrian bridge to be built over West Street that would connect with its ferry depots. The obstinate refusal of local authorities to allow this safety measure prompted an editorial in the *Railroad Gazette* on November 22, 1889:

> The West Street crossings to the various railroad ferries are so dangerous and so extremely disagreeable that it is a wonder that they have not long ago been bridged. The street is densely crowded with teams. The policemen at crossings cannot keep them clear, and the great crowds who use the ferries morning and evening pass through with real danger to life and limb. The street is also one of the dirtiest in New York City, which is the equivalent to saying that it is one of the dirtiest streets in the world.

Cassatt, of course, had to deal with this chaos each time he came to the city to dine or to conduct business or to board ship for his annual European vacation. The president of the Pennsylvania Railroad traveled from Philadelphia in his private car, with its paneled walls, Tiffany lamps, and plush red sofas. There was a gleaming brass bed in the master suite and a dining table that seated ten. But for Cassatt all luxury exclusive to his social rank ended at the Jersey City terminal, where he had to board the same ferry as everyone else and wonder in what physical condition the temperamental Hudson River would deliver him.

The mile-wide river had so exasperated Cassatt that in 1900, a year before his fateful tour of the Orléans railway extension in Paris, he had decided finally to build the Hudson River bridge. The idea of that bridge, impractical and expensive, had surfaced a number of times in the past two decades.

In 1884 Gustav Lindenthal, an Austrian-born civil engineer, proposed a triple-deck suspension bridge running from Pavonia Avenue in Jersey City and stretching across the Hudson to Desbrosses and Canal streets in Manhattan. The bridge would rise 135 feet, with a span twice that of the newly built Brooklyn Bridge. It would cost fifty-six million dollars. So desperate was the Pennsylvania Railroad for a means to conquer the Hudson that neither the highly ambitious design nor the staggering cost prevented consideration of Lindenthal's plan. The railroad sent the thirty-four-year-old bridge builder's plans to the War Department, in Washington, which had jurisdiction over structures erected on the country's navigable channels. The plans were rejected because Lindenthal's piers would have interfered with traffic on the congested river. To compound the effect of the veto, a short but severe business panic that same year wiped out all thought of investing in an expensive bridge.

Lindenthal was nonetheless determined that his bridge would be built. In 1890 he again proposed building a bridge, this one to cross the Hudson near Twenty-third Street in Manhattan, where it would feed into a terminal to be built at Sixth Avenue and Twenty-sixth Street. To this plan the War Department gave its consent, but the cost had escalated to one hundred million dollars, too much for the railroad to bear alone. The Pennsylvania agreed to build the bridge if other railroads who would benefit from it would share some of the expense, but the other rail companies withdrew from the project, and it was again shelved.

In 1892, when George B. Roberts, then president of the Pennsylvania, dispatched Samuel Rea to view the South London Railway, he also wanted Rea to come up with a plan that could be used to cross the Hudson. Rea returned not with a single plan but with five, one of which was close to

Double-deck Ferry-boat

The Pennsylvania owned a fleet of ferries like this one, which plied the Hudson between the line's Jersey City terminal and West Street.

his heart. It again called for Lindenthal's bridge, this time a double-decker carrying fourteen tracks. But, again, history dealt Lindenthal a blow; another business panic ripped the country in 1893, this time sinking it into a severe depression.

Roberts had sent Rea on his London journey after Austin Corbin, president of the Long Island Railroad, came to the Pennsylvania with a business proposal. Corbin had an idea about a tunnel.

In 1891 Corbin wanted to bring his trains into Manhattan. Once a land of potato farmers, Long Island had begun to attract city dwellers who had discovered the pleasures of country living just across the East River. When it was chartered in 1834, the railroad, which was to run up the spine of Long Island from Brooklyn to Greenport, in Suffolk County, was intended to link New York City and Boston. From Greenport a steamship would run across Long Island Sound to Stonington, Connecticut, from which another rail link would bring passengers to Boston.

This ten-hour operation ran for just four years, before an all-rail route between New York and Boston was completed in 1848, throwing the Long Island Railroad into receivership. For the next thirty-two years the Long Island became a local transportation road, desperately adding new lines as other railroad companies formed on Long Island, the competition further debilitating the troubled company. The Long Island Railroad fell into its second receivership in 1877. Three years later Austin Corbin acquired controlling stock in the company and took over the line. By 1891, the Long Island Railroad was doing a sound business handling commuters who worked in New York and lived on Long Island. But new demand for service brought need for improvements.

Like the passengers of the Pennsylvania Railroad on the Jersey shore, Long Island Railroad commuters depended on ferries to take them back and forth across the East River. Manhattan-bound passengers had to transfer from trains to ferries at a terminal in Long Island City and then cross the East River, disembarking at Thirty-fourth Street. If the ferries were inconvenient and unpleasant for commuters, the trains that brought them to the water's edge were choking Queens residents as their coal-burning locomotives spewed soot and grime into the air.

Corbin knew that the awkward, time-consuming ferry crossing would no longer serve his passengers adequately, and he had to find a better entrance to Manhattan. He hired Charles Jacobs, an English engineer with wide experience in tunnel construction, to investigate the possibility of digging under the East River to Manhattan and, at the same time, connecting Manhattan with Jersey City by tunnel. A shrewd businessman, Corbin was hoping to gain financial support for his plan from other railroads, especially the Pennsylvania.

But the depression two years later put all plans on hold. When Austin Corbin died suddenly, in June 1896, his shares of Long Island Railroad stock were placed in a five-year trust, which was due to expire on February 1, 1902. George Roberts died in 1897, but Alexander Cassatt, having become the Pennsylvania's president in 1899, saw an opportunity not only to tap the Long Island's passenger traffic but to obtain a route that would give the Pennsy access to New England. On May 9, 1900, Cassatt met with his board of directors to discuss acquiring for the Pennsylvania controlling interest in the stock of the Long Island Railroad. Cassatt told the stockholders at the annual meeting of March 1901 that securing controlling interest in the Long Island Railroad would establish a "convenient connection between your system and the New York, New Haven and Hartford Railroad Company." He said nothing more.

Cassatt was now pressed more than ever to find a means of getting his railroad into Manhattan. Once more, Lindenthal's bridge plan came out of the files. By this time, the cost of building the bridge had escalated further, and the Pennsylvania asked other railroads if they would be more amenable to financing a bridge now that the national economy had recovered. The answer was a flat no. Without further efforts at persuasion, Cassatt put away Lindenthal's plans—for good.

Just one year before Cassatt would be in Paris witnessing the opening of the Gare du Quai d'Orsay, other events were already making the possibility of tunneling under the Hudson seem practical. London was using tunnels to handle light subway traffic. In Baltimore the Baltimore and Ohio Railroad had successfully been operating trains by electricity from its Howard Street tunnel for five years. True, neither of these projects was as ambitious as the Pennsylvania's plan, but by 1901 tunnel construction methods had come a long way. Electrical power had been perfected and proven, dispelling all doubt that trains could run under rivers without depending on steam. There was a healthy business climate in the country, and the mood of industry, emerging from the shadows of a bitter depression, was expansive. And there was that bit of serendipity: Cassatt, the man of vision in charge of the Pennsylvania Railroad, had, when the opportunity arose, the foresight to purchase the Long Island Railroad.

But Cassatt would do much more than cross the Hudson. Now the Pennsylvania Railroad would burrow under two rivers, across the breadth of Manhattan. Its passengers would be able to travel across the country from California to New York City and then change trains at the new station and continue on to Montauk Point. Cassatt would not only span two rivers; he would connect a continent by rail from Pacific to Atlantic.

SCIENTIFIC AMERICAN

[Entered at the Post Office of New York, N.Y., as Second Class Matter.]

A WEEKLY JOURNAL OF PRACTICAL INFORMATION, ART, SCIENCE, MECHANICS, CHEMISTRY AND MANUFACTURES.

Vol. XLII.—No. 19.
[NEW SERIES.]

NEW YORK, MAY 8, 1880.

$3.20 per Annum.
[POSTAGE PREPAID.]

SPRINGING THE ARCH.

THE TUNNEL

INTERIOR OF THE AIR LOCK.

THE GREAT TUNNEL UNDER THE HUDSON RIVER BETWEEN NEW YORK AND NEW JERSEY.—[See page 290.]

CHAPTER FOUR

THE PLAN

I t lay buried in the mud of the riverbed, its silt-filled interior telling its own story. For six dismal months, before a specially designed caisson was sunk over the break, the unfinished tunnel was a tomb. Twenty years later the tragedy that occurred not far from his Jersey City ferry slips reminded Cassatt of the high price of failure.

In 1874 De Witt Haskin, a former Union army colonel and mining entrepreneur, organized the Hudson River Tunnel Company to build a railroad tunnel under the Hudson. Haskin's tunnel would begin at Fifteenth Street in Jersey City and come out in Manhattan at Morton Street. Eventually this ambitious scheme was to bring the tunnel under the streets of Manhattan to Washington Square, where Haskin planned a great station for all the railroads whose lines stopped at the New Jersey waterfront. Coincidentally Haskin's tunnel paralleled the route taken by the Lackawanna Railroad's Christopher Street ferry. The coincidence was too much for the Lackawanna, which feared the competition greatly enough to secure a court injunction against the tunnel, halting all work. The railroad claimed that Haskin's tunnel project infringed on their property rights. For five years Haskin's tunnel rested in limbo; then the injunction was lifted and work resumed. But the project, overambitious and poorly financed, now showed signs of bad planning and technical ignorance. Haskin's experience with railroad tunnels was limited to hard-rock mining in the West. He knew nothing about tunneling under a river and had little knowledge of the Hudson's soft riverbed.

On the morning of July 21, 1880, Haskin's men entered the shaft at Jersey City to begin excavating an enlarged permanent entrance from the shaft to the two tunnels. The men descended in caissons and then entered air locks where they would wait until twelve pounds of air pressure developed. From there they would open the tunnel door and begin cutting away at the soft soil. All was well as long as the men did not hit any of the treacherous water pockets that turned the soft mud to liquid. It was imperative that the silt be thick enough to keep the pressurized air from escaping.

But this morning the mud was incredibly soft, much too soft to hold back the air. Pete Woodland, an assistant engineer, was the first to see the tiny leak in the earth. He dropped his tools, sounded the alarm, and raced toward the air lock, shouting to his men. Eight workers ran out into the

The engineers planning Cassatt's tunnels worked in the shadow of a calamitous failure of twenty years earlier. Not long after this issue of Scientific American *reported on the progress of De Witt Haskin's tunnel, water poured in and drowned twenty workmen.*

47

air lock as he held the door open. Suddenly, the tiny leak exploded into a gush, and the river rushed into the tunnel, instantly flooding it. Woodland, who could have been the first into the air lock, instead slammed the door shut from outside. It was an instinctive decision, made with no thought to personal consequences. The men within the air lock heard the river waters roar down on Woodland and his fellow workers still trapped inside the tunnel. Eight men survived to tell the story. For Pete Woodland and nineteen others the tunnel became a tomb.

Twenty years after the tragic blowout, the ghosts of those men hovered about the Pennsylvania Railroad's project. On the day the railroad announced its tunnel plans, Cassatt appointed a commission of engineers, all experts in their fields, to inform him of the best and safest way to build.

The first of the experts was Charles M. Jacobs, the British-born tunnel engineer whom Austin Corbin had hired to draft plans for bringing the Long Island Railroad under the East River. Second was Charles W. Raymond, a colonel in the Army Corps of Engineers whom Cassatt appointed chairman of the board of engineers in charge of the Pennsylvania's New York tunnel extension.

Raymond's assistant was William Brown, chief engineer of the Pennsylvania Railroad. Next came Alfred Noble, an expert in bridge and canal construction, recently honored by President William McKinley with an appointment to the Isthmian Canal Commission. Then there was Gustav Lindenthal, whose bridge would never be built but whose fifteen years' experience with the Pennsylvania Railroad would be an invaluable asset. Finally, George Gibbs, an electrical engineer specializing in motive power, would be in charge of electric traction and the new station contruction. These six men would report to Samuel Rea, who in turn would bring their findings to Cassatt. From the outset they were told that cost was no object, that the safest and best methods of tunneling under the Hudson were what the Pennsylvania wanted from them.

The plan was to bring the line across the Hackensack Meadow, then over a high landfill to a place called Bergen Hill, where two separate single-track tunnels would begin burrowing under the Hudson, coming out in Manhattan at Tenth Avenue between Thirty-first and Thirty-third streets. The tracks would remain below street level and would increase from two to twenty-one as they fed into the new station, to be located between Seventh and Eighth avenues.

On the Long Island side, four single-track tunnels would extend from Long Island City, dipping into the East River in four separate tubes at the Sunnyside Yards. Once in Manhattan, the trains would make their way under the city through the four tunnels until they came to Pennsylvania Station.

As if he were drawing up a battle plan, Cassatt immediately apportioned the work into four divisions. The Meadows Division would extend from the Manhattan Transfer—the proposed railroad station near Harrison, New Jersey, where trains would switch from steam to electric locomotives—to the tunnel portals at the mouth of the Hudson. William Brown was placed in charge. The North River Division, headed by Charles Jacobs, would carry the trains through Bergen Hill, then under the river and out again to Tenth Avenue in Manhattan. The East River Division would bring trains under the city from Seventh Avenue eastward beneath the East River to connect finally with a Long Island line. Alfred Noble, who headed this division, was also in charge of Sunnyside Yard, in Long Island City, a 206-acre maintenance area where Pennsy trains would be cleaned and serviced. The last segment of work, known as the Electric Traction and Station Construction Division, with George Gibbs in charge, was responsible for the electrification of the tracks as well as construction of the steel shell for the new station.

Part of Cassatt's great ambition to bring his railroad east was to build a bridge to carry passengers and freight into New England. The plan had actually been drawn up by April 21, 1892, when the Pennsylvania and the New Haven roads went into partnership to form the New York Connecting Railroad Company. Out of this union would come a bridge to be built over Hell Gate, a narrow strait one hundred feet deep that separates Queens from the northeastern edge of Manhattan. In the nineteenth century ships used the pass as a shortcut to Boston, eliminating thirty-eight miles of the circuitous route around Long Island by braving the swift crosscurrents and outcroppings of jagged rock that earned the strait its name.

Cassatt was not planning to use the new Hudson River tunnels to carry freight. Freight cars would be ferried on car floats across the Hudson from New Jersey to Brooklyn, where they could be coupled to locomotives for the trip across the New York Connecting Bridge, which would carry the freight trains to the New Haven tracks for the trip north. Passengers arriving at Penn Station from the south and west could continue on to New England and as far north as Canada by way of the bridge as well. But the course that had to be navigated to get the bridge built proved as treacherous as the waters of Hell Gate itself. The plan Cassatt submitted on January 18, 1906, would not be realized until 1917, seven years after Pennsylvania Station was completed.

While construction of the New York Connecting Bridge was still in the distant future, the Pennsylvania Railroad's tunnel plans were close to realization. But these too were carefully scrutinized, and proper planning was never sacrificed to haste. Before the first shovel was plunged into earth, Cassatt's engineers would work for two years at their drafting tables, reviewing and revising each phase of every plan. Later when sandhogs went to work inside the tunnels, Cassatt took elaborate safety precautions to safeguard them. The lesson of the Haskin tunnel was not lost on him.

In the meantime Cassatt had other railroad matters to attend to, not the least of which was a bit of friendly competition with the Pennsylvania's chief rival, the New York Central.

For fifteen years, as far back as 1887, the Pennsylvania Railroad had been engaged in a race with the New York Central for supremacy in the highly lucrative New York–Chicago run. In 1887 the *Pennsylvania Special*, one of the first of the Pennsylvania Flyers, was introduced with sleeping cars, a library-buffet car, and other amenities never before seen on a train. Eleven years later the Pennsylvania declared all-out war on Cornelius Vanderbilt's railroad, ordering more powerful locomotives designed for greater speed and Pullman cars that resembled the coaches of royalty. The green-and-scarlet luxury flyers were equipped with observation cars finished in walnut, mahogany, and English oak.

The age of the luxury train had arrived. By the turn of the century, railroading was much more than a means to get from one place to another. It was, as Jacques Barzun has written, "an institution, an image of man, a tradition, a code of honor, a source of poetry, a nursery of boyhood desires, a sublimest of toys, and the most solemn machine—next to the funeral hearse—that marks the epochs of man's life." Certainly these new super trains, through which one could view, from morning into night, the vast expanse that was America, were poems in motion. Glittering palaces on wheels, with more conveniences inside their close quarters than could be had in most European homes, luxury passenger cars were images of national self-perception. And in true American spirit, the best was yet to come.

In winter 1902, while Cassatt was organizing his board of engineers for the new tunnels, William Newman, president of the New York Central,

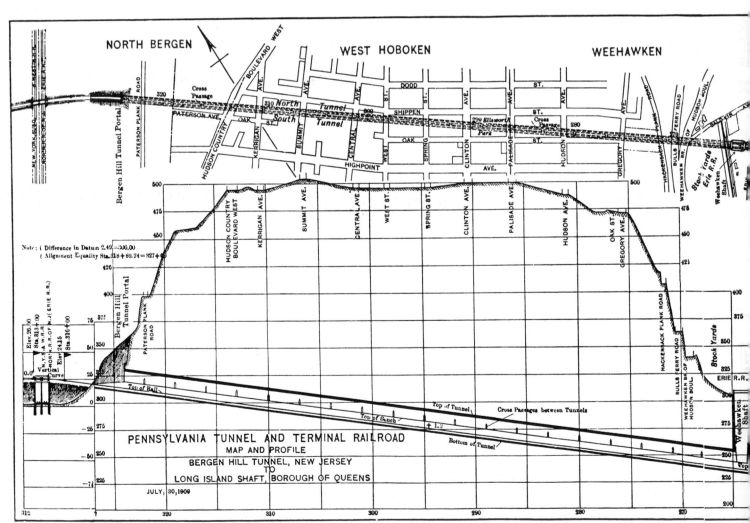

announced that his railroad would make the New York–Chicago run in
twenty hours. This meant that 980 miles of track would be covered at an
average rate of 50 miles per hour. The speed and the distance were not
particularly startling; in 1893 the New York Central's *Empire State Express*
traveled well over 100 miles an hour, and during that same year the
Exposition Flyer, a New York Central experimental train, had taken passengers
from Manhattan to Chicago in twenty hours. What was novel about Newman's
announcement was that the New York Central's new train would run on
a daily schedule.

This train of beautiful appointments, crisp efficiency, and incomparable
speed would be given a name suitable to the railroad's thrust into the future:
the *Twentieth Century Limited*. It would not be a train for the average
passenger.

The prosperous traveler would walk across a red carpet to board at Chicago,
leave the city at twelve-thirty in the afternoon, take meals—dinner alongside
Lake Erie, breakfast by the Hudson—prepared by superb chefs, and, refreshed

*A contemporary map shows, at top,
the Pennsylvania Railroad's route
from North Bergen, New Jersey, to
Manhattan and, below, a profile
of the terrain the tunnels had
to bore through.*

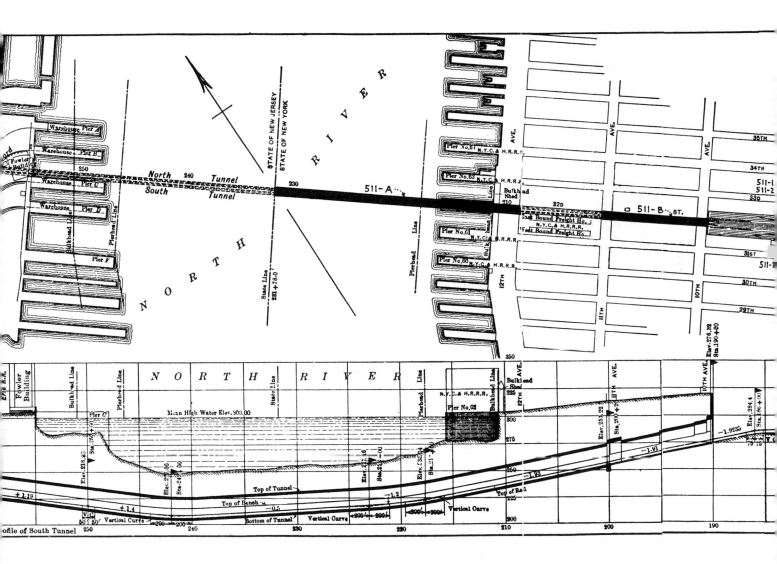

from a night's sleep in a nicely-appointed roomette, would arrive in midtown Manhattan at nine-thirty in the morning: plenty of time to put in a day on Wall Street or get over to the Hudson docks to board a White Star liner for Europe.

As all the New York Central's trains had done for the past thirty years, the *Twentieth Century Limited* would come into Manhattan over Spuyten Duyvil Creek, having crossed the Hudson up north over a bridge at Albany. It would then roll down Fourth Avenue through Harlem, over a viaduct to Ninety-sixth Street, where it would descend into a tunnel and then out again through a brick-walled trench below street level, approaching Grand Central's train shed through a smoky landscape of maintenance yards and engine sheds that extended from Forty-ninth Street to Forty-fifth Street behind the "headhouse," the passenger area of the terminal.

Well aware of the New York Central's plans, the Pennsylvania Railroad was busy working on its own supertrain. It, too, would be the latest in luxury, and it would make the New York–Chicago run in the same twenty

The continuation of the map on the preceding pages follows the route through Pennsylvania Station, across Manhattan's East Side, and under the East River to Queens—the tunnels the Long Island Railroad trains used. At top right, that road's Sunnyside yards.

BOROUGH OF MANHATTAN

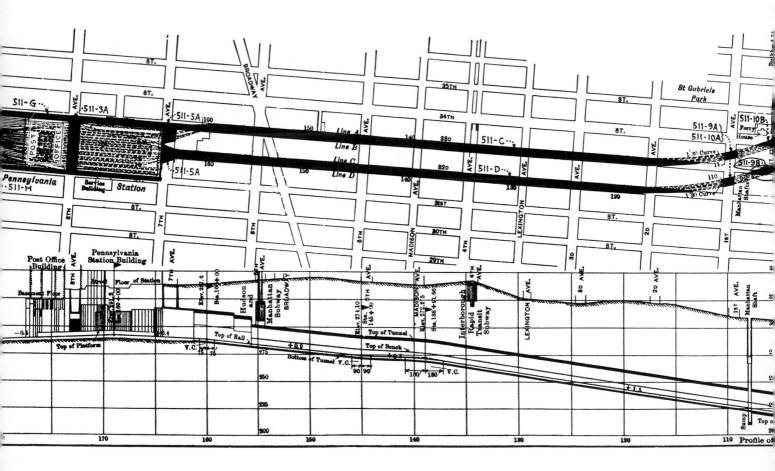

hours. To accommodate the new high-speed train and its future sister fleet, the Pennsylvania installed an automatic signaling system along its tracks between its Philadelphia and Jersey City stations, enabling the faster train to pass slower locals by diverting it onto freight tracks and returning it to the regular tracks when the local had passed. On March 24 a two-car special carrying Alexander Cassatt made a nonstop run from Broad Street Station in Philadelphia to the terminal in Jersey City, a distance of almost ninety

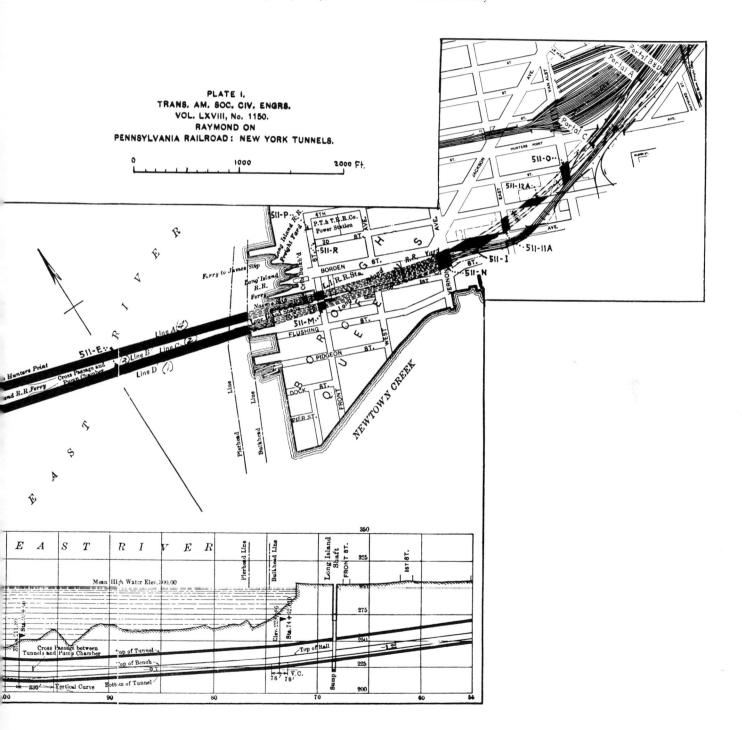

PLATE I.
TRANS. AM. SOC. CIV. ENGRS.
VOL. LXVIII, No. 1150.
RAYMOND ON
PENNSYLVANIA RAILROAD: NEW YORK TUNNELS.

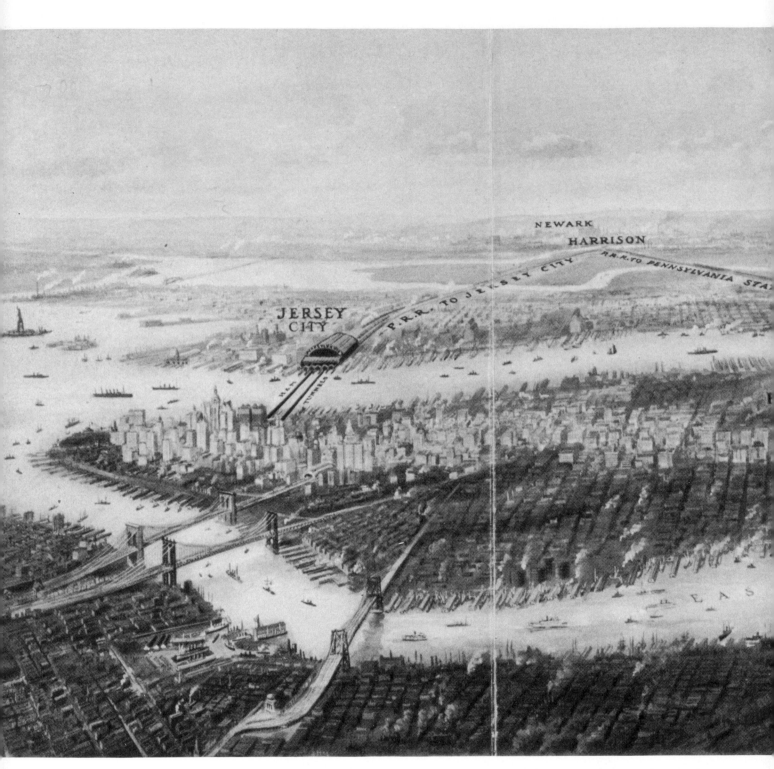

Pennsylvania Station shines in the center of this splendid 1910 aerial view, which looks west from Long Island, across Manhattan, to New Jersey.

The "shield method" of tunnel construction in operation: as the great iron cylinder inched forward, sandhogs hauled the rock and mud it displaced back through the tunnel they were building.

miles, at sixty-eight miles per hour, demonstrating for the first time the possibilities of sustained high speed under the new automatic signals.

Cassatt had to be more than satisfied with his train's performance. But it was not until early summer that the real test would occur. The man who loved a good horse race was about to watch one of the most exciting races of his life. Both the New York Central and the Pennsylvania Railroad decided to inaugurate their supertrains on June 16, 1902. On that day and each day thereafter the two trains would leave for Chicago at exactly the same time. Yet this race was unusual; it was not won at the finish line. Speed was important here but not paramount. This was a race of prestige to see which train would become dearer to America.

The Pennsylvania's entry was called the *Pennsylvania Special,* a name inherited from the line's first luxury flyers of fifteen years before. It would make the New York–Chicago run for ten years before it received a new name, more appropriate to its glamour: the *Broadway Limited.*

On that June day the *Twentieth Century* departed from Grand Central while the *Pennsylvania Special* began its run from Jersey City. The *Pennsylvania Special* traveled northwest, over more rugged terrain; it crossed the Alleghenies and had to negotiate the famous Horseshoe Curve near Altoona, Pennsylvania. The *Twentieth Century* traveled due north, but if its route

56

was smoother than that of the competition, it was also more circuitous. Both trains went their separate ways until they reached the outskirts of Chicago, where the Central's tracks paralleled those of the Pennsylvania.

It was on that six-mile stretch that the trains, on their return journey from Chicago, raced each other. They departed daily from their stations —the *Pennsylvania Special* out of Union Station and the *Twentieth Century* out of LaSalle Street Station—at exactly 12:40 P.M., coming alongside each other at Englewood, Illinois, seven and a half miles outside of Chicago, and then rocketing along for six miles to the delight of passengers and crew.

On June 17, 1902, the day after the *Pennsylvania Special's* inaugural run, the *New York Times* reported that its westbound section had been on time but its eastbound section was two minutes late due to a runaway freight car that the *Special* had to push two miles to the nearest siding.

The supertrains were an instant success for both railroads. The famous New York–Chicago run of the *Twentieth Century* and what would later be called the *Broadway Limited* became an indestructible American emblem within a generation. In 1933 Ben Hecht and Charles MacArthur would write a hit Broadway show called *Twentieth Century*, and later the Pennsylvania Railroad would prod Hollywood to shoot a film about their star train titled, of course, *Broadway Limited*. Paintings of the trains made for the calendars of both railroad companies would hang in museums. The Pennsylvania Railroad commissioned one of the most famous, Griff Teller's *Broadway Meets the Dawn*.

But for Cassatt this new beauty race was a thrill tinged with frustration: victory was lost at the riverbank. Unlike the *Twentieth Century* Cassatt's train had no red carpet rolled out in an elegant new terminal. Passengers boarding the Pennsylvania supertrain still had to endure the damnable river crossing. No wonder Cassatt watched with consuming interest as his engineers plotted their attack.

After much study it was decided that the "shield method" would be used for tunneling under the rivers. The shield was a giant iron cylinder, slightly larger than the tunnel being built, which would protect the work under construction and assist in the building of the iron shell that would form the tunnel itself. In the front of the shield were nine doors through which the rock, sand, and silt of the riverbed passed. Behind the shield cast-iron plates two and a half feet in length were bolted together to form an iron ring. As each ring was put in place, excavation was done ahead of the shield and the shield pushed forward into the area excavated so that another ring could be erected. Each ring was flanged so that it could be bolted to the next ring. The resulting series of rings formed the shell of the tunnel.

It was a painstaking process. In the Bergen Hill Tunnels Cassatt's men would bore only six feet a day through obdurate traprock. But the method would be safe (as safe as any known to engineering), and that for Cassatt was more important than speed. However, the day when his ferries would go into dry dock, the day when his *Pennsylvania Special* would race through the tunnels and enter Manhattan (and a new station), was a long way off. Before any ribbon-cutting ceremonies, men would have to tunnel through the hardest of traprock at Bergen Hill and the softest of mud under the Hudson. Cassatt would have to face danger, disappointment, and even tragedy.

CHAPTER FIVE

UNDER THE RIVER
WITH THE SANDHOGS

Each day groups of them met at the river's edge on Thirty-second Street, where the Pennsylvania's *Victor* ferried them across the Hudson. They would disembark at King's Bluff, in Weehawken, site of Hamilton and Burr's infamous duel, and then make their way past a mountain of iron castings and great hills of cement to the Weehawken shaft.

The three engineers who led the sandhogs had built tunnels in South America and South Africa, and one of them had come directly from helping make the original Aswan Dam, on the Nile. They were the best-qualified tunnel engineers in the world, and they would lead armies of men through blasted rock into the dark mudholes that were to become the Hudson River tunnels.

In accordance with Cassatt's plans, the work began on both sides of the river at approximately the same time, each army burrowing through the riverbed until they met in the center.

The mouth of the Weehawken shaft was 100 feet wide and 154 feet long. Workers descended 76 feet to its bottom in a tiny cage. At the entrance to the shaft a small village of machine shops, workshops, and a smithy fashioned and maintained the presses, drills, and lathes. Inside an engine room, an enormous machine pumped life into the curious underground organism into whose bowels the sandhogs descended. Next to the engine room was the boiler room, where stokers shoveled coal into three 500-horsepower boilers. Thundering air compressors supplied the tunnels with the pressurized air that prevented cave-in. All of this apparatus was duplicated across the Hudson at the site of the Manhattan shaft.

The realm of the river bottom was like none on the earth's surface. The bottom of the Weehawken shaft was an intersection at which all the traffic from the tunnels would converge. To the east were the twin tubes that would become the Hudson River tunnels; to the west the beginning of the tunnels under Bergen Hill, a beginning that stretched from Weehawken to the portal that would penetrate the surface of Hackensack Meadow.

On the New Jersey side, four hundred and fifty men working in two 10-hour shifts blasted away at traprock, basalt of unyielding hardness. They drilled holes into the rock at the face of the tunnel and inserted dynamite. With the sticks in place, a powderman gave a warning shout: "Fire!" Then the explosion ripped through the tunnel, bringing with it a thick blanket

Far beneath the East River, sandhogs pause a moment for the photographer in the fall of 1906. The picture shows the cast iron plates that were bolted together in concentric rings—one every two and a half feet—to form the tunnel's shell.

of acrid smoke. After the dust settled, the sandhogs loaded the blasted rock onto carts called electric mules and sent them through the tunnel back to the shaft. All along the way the din of hammers hit against hard rock mixed with the ominous hiss of escaping air.

The work in the Bergen Hill tunnels was tedious and unmercifully slow. The average daily advance into the tunnels was only about eight and a half feet, and the amount of preparation time for each attack at the rock was thirty-six hours. At one point, on the Weehawken side, the tunnel advanced beneath an old warehouse that sat on an enormous number of long piles, each of which had to be cut, a procedure not only delicate but extremely hazardous.

Unlike the Bergen Hill tunnels those under the Hudson were not blasted through rock but formed in the soft riverbed. Here, in the shifting, unpredictable mud, the more serious danger lay.

At the tunnel's entrance was dripping water, intense darkness, and deafening noise. Men seemed to be everywhere in what looked like mass confusion. Some, faces darkened with grime, peered wearily at those who had not yet begun their shift. The whites of the eyes of exhausted workers gave them the look of stalking demons. Farther into the tunnel, the harsh glow of a string of electric lights led to an iron wall with three massive doors. A valve was turned, and one of the doors opened. From behind the door, an eerie roar: no Minotaur, only the air blasting out of the air lock.

When the roar subsided the door leading to a small iron room was opened wide. Workers filed in to sit on a narrow bench. The door was shut, another valve was turned, and a loud hiss filled the entire space. For a few seconds, compressed air surged into the compartment. Then the sandhogs inside relieved the pressure building on their eardrums by pinching their nostrils, closing their mouths, and blowing until ears popped clear. As more air entered the air lock the pressure eventually reached the same level as that of the tunnel. It was this compressed air that prevented devastating blowouts.

With equal pressure achieved, the inner door opposite the first one was opened, admitting the men into the working chamber of the tunnel. Here the light dimmed, and in the tomblike atmosphere the workmen looked less like free citizens of a New World than slaves building a monument to an ancient god. A succession of cast-iron rings formed a gigantic tube through which the men passed. Underfoot was a timber floor with two lines of narrow tracks. On one, cars containing cast-iron segments ran down toward the tunnel head; on the other, a huge rope pulled cars loaded with black mud toward the air lock.

As the crew got closer to the tunnel head they could see more men—sometimes forty or fifty—working constantly. It was here that the great shield, weighing two hundred tons, stood between the tunnel and the riverbed. Each day this reluctant giant edged forward two and a half feet at a time. Occasionally when the shield was shoved ahead, all of its doors were closed so that none of the muck it moved through was brought into the tunnel. But usually at least one door was left open to facilitate the pushing: mud would stream in through the door in a semiliquid mass that resembled a monstrous sausage.

While the shield was going forward and mud was flowing into the tunnel, cars were run up as close behind as possible on both tracks, and any man who was not pushing the shield shoveled mud into the cars. When all the mud was cleared away, another cast-iron ring was erected next to the last. In the beginning it took the sandhogs five to six hours to put a single ring in place. By the time the work was in full progress they could put one up in thirty minutes. Nevertheless, the process was still tedious and dangerous.

For the sandhog, however, the greatest danger occurred when his shift ended and he had to leave the atmosphere of compressed air to enter the world above the water. While he was working in compressed air the sandhog often experienced a feeling of well-being, a kind of pleasant high, as nitrogen bubbles danced through his bloodstream. But when he passed from compressed to normal air the tissues lying near the surface of the skin gave off the nitrogen bubbles quite readily while the visceral organs—heart and kidneys especially—and sometimes the spinal column retained the gas. When the body was returned too quickly to normal air conditions the retained gas exerted pressure on the nerves and nerve centers, causing pain so intense that men doubled up and, in their agony, twisted into the distorted positions that gave the disease "the bends" its name. When the pressure was in the spinal column, unconsciousness sometimes resulted, and a man could lapse into coma. Even when a doctor was able to bring the victim to, partial or complete paralysis could occur. In some cases movement was restored after several years, but in many instances the paralysis was permanent.

Sandhogs stand triumphantly at the doors of the shield in one of the Hudson tunnels in 1908: their work is done, the tunnel is completed, the shield is soon to be dismantled and removed.

SMITHSONIAN INSTITUTION

Alexander Cassatt knew of the problem. A few years before, Washington Roebling had contracted the bends while building the Brooklyn Bridge. The disease turned him into a recluse who directed the completion of his famous bridge from a window in his Brooklyn Heights home. It was not just Roebling. Over one hundred men working in the caissons for the bridge were stricken with the bends. Several died.

Cassatt made extraordinary efforts to protect his sandhogs during the construction of the tunnels. Each man's locker was heated to ensure that any wet clothes placed inside would be dry for the next wearing. Hot and cold baths were readied for men when they ended their shifts. Hot coffee was always on tap in large quantities; tunnel coffee, as it was called, was thought to be an antidote to the effects of compressed air. In addition to the air locks inside the tunnels, "hospital" locks were installed at the surface of each shaft in case a sandhog left the tunnel with signs of the bends. The hospital lock was divided into two compartments, one of which allowed a doctor to enter and leave any time. Inside the lock were mattresses, thermometers, blood-pressure gauges—everything a doctor needed to keep a careful watch on his patient. These precautions were set up at both the New Jersey and the Manhattan shafts.

The Manhattan shaft intersected the work on the Hudson River tunnels proceeding west and the tunneling from the river's edge to the new Pennsylvania Station. In contrast to the hard, unyielding rock that was Bergen Hill, the foundation under New York is a softer, more penetrable substance known as mica schist. But the very properties that make it easy to penetrate also caused it to break off and collapse into the tunnels. An elaborate support system had to be built to keep the rock from crashing through the tunnel walls.

By September 1904 all of Cassatt's tunnels were under way, including those beneath the East River, which had been started four months earlier. It was apparent now that the invasion of New York by the Pennsylvania Railroad was imminent, but the great railroad was not alone in conquering the Hudson, and it would not, after all this, be the first to do so.

Downriver, at the site of the old Haskin tunnel and without much fanfare, history was being made. On March 11, 1904, six months before Cassatt's sandhogs first entered the shafts, Charles Jacobs, the man who would head the work for Cassatt in the Hudson River tunnels, became the first man to walk below the Hudson.

In 1892 William Gibbs McAdoo, a young, ambitious Georgia lawyer with entrepreneurial talents, saw in the relic that was once the Haskin tunnel a potentially good investment. After Pete Woodland's tragic death in 1880, work had continued on the Haskin tunnel despite a series of blowouts, cave-ins, and financial setbacks. By the time the project was finally abandoned in 1891, two tunnels had been begun from both sides of the Hudson. The longest was the north tunnel from New Jersey, with nearly four thousand feet completed.

Impressed by Jacobs's reputation and accomplishments, McAdoo contacted Cassatt's chief engineer. Jacobs had not only advised Austin Corbin on the feasibility of a tunnel for the Long Island Railroad, he had also built a gas tunnel between Ravenswood, Long Island, and Seventy-first Street in Manhattan. That tunnel, which ran under Blackwell's Island, in the East River, had posed engineering challenges so difficult that the original contractors had abandoned it. Jacobs finished it under near-impossible conditions.

When Jacobs proclaimed Haskin's abortive tunnel sound, McAdoo formed the Hudson and Manhattan Railroad Company. In the summer of 1902, two years before the Pennsylvania Railroad's work started, construction on the H&M tunnels began. Rather than use the Haskin method of caissons to build the tunnels, Jacobs employed the shield, the same method that would be used in the Pennsylvania's tunnels.

McAdoo's tunnels would extend from Hoboken, New Jersey, to Sixth Avenue at Washington Square. There they would turn northward to a station at Thirty-third Street. Unlike the Pennsylvania's tunnels, McAdoo's would be used exclusively by commuter trains traveling between New York and New Jersey. Years later these would be dubbed PATH (for Port Authority Trans-Hudson) trains.

McAdoo's tunnels reached Manhattan in 1908, two years before the Pennsylvania trains could enter their new terminal. Alexander Cassatt may have contributed indirectly to the success of McAdoo's plan. In December 1901, when he announced his railroad's plans, Cassatt made it clear that the Pennsylvania's Hudson River tunnels were intended for long-distance passenger travel. The average commuter traveling between Manhattan and New Jersey would still have to depend on ferries. Demonstrating the need for tunnels to accommodate commuters as well, McAdoo was able to convince financial backers to invest in his plan.

To New Yorkers it hardly mattered who got there first. More important was that the island of Manhattan was no longer isolated from the rest of the country. It was finally linked to every other city served by rail.

First the Roeblings built their Brooklyn Bridge, joining Manhattan with Brooklyn and offering an alternative to the ferries that ran between the two boroughs. Now there was talk of abandoning the ferries that brought people back and forth from New York to Long Island and replacing them with tunnels. New Yorkers had to wonder how all of this would change the place in which they lived. Cassatt, too, wondered just how this provincial, sophisticated, tough, and beautiful city would receive him.

CHAPTER SIX

A PALACE IN HELL'S KITCHEN

The city into which Alexander Cassatt was finally bringing his railroad stood on the verge of tremendous change. Like other major cities in America, New York was straining toward the future, and Gotham coming into the twentieth century was an exciting thing to see.

Yet much of the city belonged to the century it was leaving behind. Washington Square, with its elegant, tree-shaded town houses, still reflected the genteel world of Henry James. The Renaissance mansions and beautiful churches of McKim, Mead and White along Madison and Fifth avenues had the staid air of invulnerable, everlasting wealth.

But with increasing frequency, buildings taller and more ambitious than anyone might have expected rose above the brownstones and the church spires, lifting the eye skyward. The American skyscraper, steel-framed and sleek, came into its own in the 1890s, and by 1901 the twenty-story Fuller Building, nicknamed the Flatiron because of its prowlike shape, was erected on Twenty-third Street between Broadway and Fifth Avenue, standing tall against the five- and six-story buildings that surrounded it.

Electricity was also changing the face of New York and the way New Yorkers traveled their city. The elevated lines that ran along four of Manhattan's avenues would soon retire their steam locomotives in favor of the new electric cars. Below them electric trolleys were already nudging the plodding horsecars into memory. And below the trolley cars, a tunnel was being bored for Manhattan's first subway. Down at City Hall Theodore Roosevelt, then governor of the state, had broken ground for August Belmont's grand ambition. The new Interboro Rapid Transit Subway would begin at City Hall, running north with only one express stop before reaching Forty-second Street, or, more precisely, Grand Central Station.

This building, newly transformed from the former Grand Central Depot, must have stirred within Cassatt both admiration and envy. In 1901 work was completed on rebuilding the New York Central's depot. The red brick walls, with their cast-iron embellishments, were stripped and resurfaced with a handsome granite, and the three mansard roofs were removed. Inside the building, which had grown from three to six stories, passengers were awed by a central waiting room with a steel-ribbed skylight rising fifty feet. This room of steel and glass told them in no uncertain terms that they

One of the first skyscrapers in Manhattan, the Flatiron Building was just three years old when this picture was taken in 1905. Rising twenty-one stories from its wedge of land, the building, said one critic, was an "ocean steamer with all Broadway in tow."

65

Noisy with commerce and the constant clatter of elevated trains, the Bowery in 1903 was less glamorous than it had been a generation earlier, but among Manhattan's thoroughfares, it was still second in fame only to Broadway. We are looking uptown from Grand Street.

were in a railroad station. Incorporating three separate stations into one terminal, the building was rechristened Grand Central Station.

In 1869, after having consolidated the New York Central and Hudson River railroads with his Harlem River Railroad, Cornelius Vanderbilt began building a depot that would serve all three lines. For the site he chose Forty-second Street and Fourth Avenue, where the Harlem and New Haven railroads already had their locomotive maintenance shops. When Vanderbilt erected his new depot, Forty-second Street was considered the northernmost bastion of civilization. With the establishment of houses of worship several blocks above Forty-second Street, there were hints that the city's wealthy families would soon venture north along Madison and Fifth avenues, but the East Side was still generally crowded with tenements and breweries, serving Irish and German immigrants. To the north small farms and an occasional row of shingle houses signaled the urban boundary.

Actually, even if consolidation had not been on his mind Vanderbilt would have been restricted to an uptown location. He had already been forced to move his Harlem River Railroad uptown when New York City's Common Council decreed in 1856 that because of the noise, dirt, and threat of danger, no steam locomotives could travel in Manhattan south of Forty-second Street. Cornelius Vanderbilt was said to be so concerned about his new depot's remote location that he made sure the passenger entrance faced south, where most civilized activity lay.

This was a time when twenty-nine years in New York City was like a century almost anyplace else, and Forty-second Street's progress raced with the jerky movements of a silent movie. A few blocks west of Grand Central Station, on Fifth Avenue, the pastoral Croton Reservoir had come down to make way for the New York Public Library. Farther west Oscar Hammerstein had just opened his famous vaudeville theater, the Victoria, on the corner of Broadway and Forty-second. It was a fitting climax to the parade of theaters that had been marching up Broadway's rialto for the past half-century. They started at Madison Square at Twenty-sixth Street, where the gilded Diana, said to be modeled after Stanford White's mistress, Evelyn Nesbitt, perched atop his Madison Square Garden. By 1901 the rialto had reached Forty-second Street, and with the new electric street lamps lighting up the night, it became known as the Great White Way.

Not far from the Victoria, on a triangular patch of land that had been part of the Longacre, a forlorn area once the home of the American Horse Exchange, a tower rising 375 feet was being built to house the *New York Times*. August Belmont's subway would make a stop here, and since he liked to have his stations named after noteworthy structures nearby, why not name this one after the new Times Tower and call it Times Square? The twentieth century had come to Forty-second Street, and the street that was referred to as the End of the World when Vanderbilt put his depot there had now become the Crossroads of the World.

Unlike Grand Central, Cassatt's railroad station would be located in an area that had not known much change, at least not architecturally. The edifice of poverty is a death mask, neither reflecting life nor recording its disintegration, and in 1901 the West Side of Manhattan, especially where

Opposite: Cassatt's rival road, the New York Central, enjoyed the enormous advantage of having a station in midtown—Grand Central, seen here in 1900.

Below: In the most elegant event ever to take place in a New York City subway station Mayor George McClellan (with the white beard) and a group of dignitaries inaugurate the first IRT train at City Hall station in February 1904.

MUSEUM OF THE CITY OF NEW YORK

Right: The half-finished Times Tower dominated the view north toward Times Square in 1904.

Below: The reformer Jacob Riis photographed this street in Hell's Kitchen, the dispiriting neighborhood where Cassatt would build his palatial station.

it hugged the Hudson River, was a Dickensian landscape of piano factories, stockyards, and slaughterhouses. Rows of tenements housed people who lived amid the stench of slaughtered pigs and cattle. Thirty-ninth Street, the hub of this noisome activity, was nicknamed Abattoir Place or Pig Alley. Above the streets an ever-present dense gray cloud of soot, spewed from the chimneys of freighters and ocean liners that clogged the piers, darkened the sun. It mixed with coal smoke from freight trains that ran along Eleventh Avenue and from the elevated trains that ran above Ninth.

The freight trains belonged to several railroads, including the Pennsylvania's chief rival, the New York Central. In 1851 Erastus Corning built a depot between Thirtieth and Thirty-first streets and Tenth and Eleventh avenues to accommodate passengers on his Hudson River Railroad, which ran from Canal Street in Manhattan northward along the eastern shore of the Hudson River to East Albany. Gradually other railroads dotted the waterfront with their warehouses and freight terminals. Cornelius Vanderbilt, who acquired the Hudson River Railroad in 1864, scoffed at people who thought it unwise to build a rail line in an unpopulated part of the city. "Put the road there," he is credited with saying, "and people will go there to live." And they did. And with them came all the side effects of industrial poverty. What was once part of the Eden Farm, a bucolic stretch of hills penetrated by clear streams, was now covered with a network of railroad tracks running north and south along Tenth, Eleventh, and Twelfth avenues. Distilleries, glue factories, and the infamous slaughterhouses spread over the land. Then came the jerry-built tenements to house the workers. Children played in streets where the carcasses of dead horses were left to rot. Eleventh Avenue, with Vanderbilt's constant run of freight trains chugging through the neighborhood at street level, became known as Death Avenue.

Gangs of hoodlums sprang predictably from the impotent chaos there, so angry and bloodthirsty that the area once called Bloemendael, or Vale of Flowers, became known as Hell's Kitchen. This neighborhood, locked into poverty for fifty years, would be the northwest border of Cassatt's new railroad station. Below it the country-village charm that was Chelsea had taken the spillover from Hell's Kitchen. Town houses became rooming houses, and the sound of horse hooves over cobblestone was replaced by the rattle of the Ninth Avenue el.

In Manhattan, neighborhoods can end abruptly at street curbs, and the width of an avenue may be the difference between defeat and hope. Unfortunately for Cassatt, not even the frontier defined by two avenues could mark a change. To the east of Hell's Kitchen and Chelsea, along the new station's Seventh Avenue border, the remnants of the infamous Tenderloin clung obstinately, the last guests at a party that had begun twenty years before when this red light district, sometimes called Satan's Circus, had sprung up between Fifth and Seventh avenues from Fourteenth to Forty-second streets. Brownstones were openly used as brothels, and pimps blatantly conducted their business in public, all sanctioned by the Tammany Hall politicians who ran the city.

On Sunday morning, February 14, 1892, the Reverend Charles H. Parkhurst mounted the pulpit of Madison Square Presbyterian Church, designed by Stanford White, and preached his famous Saint Valentine's

Day sermon, denouncing the ladies of sin and all those who profited from them. After some thunder and lightning the district became somewhat more subdued, although it still operated, if not as openly, for all who cared to visit. By the time Cassatt was ready to build his railroad station, many of the notorious clubs and dance halls were gone, and the wholesale flower market had begun to take root. Still, the Tenderloin continued to exist, if no longer so strongly in fact, most definitely in the minds of New Yorkers.

It was into this world of aging slums and tired brothels that Cassatt would introduce his pink granite temple. He would require twenty-eight acres, an enormous amount of ground, before his project was complete. The station alone would rise on eight of those acres, two city blocks, and the path from the station to the water's edge would raze an entire neighborhood.

Unlike Vanderbilt's Grand Central, Cassatt's new station would not lie at the Crossroads of the World. It was true that, farther east, Thirty-fourth Street had reaped some of the benefits of Manhattan's move uptown. The theaters, show palaces, and hotels that ran up Broadway were glittering more than ever. On the corner of Thirty-fourth Street and Fifth Avenue the wealthy held court at the opulent Waldorf-Astoria, with its celebrated Peacock Alley. Farther west McKim, Mead and White's famous Herald Building straddled Broadway and Sixth Avenue as the cornerstone of an emerging Herald Square. But how could this activity affect Cassatt's new railroad station, which was distanced from it all by a long stretch of avenue? One bit of news gave Cassatt cause for optimism: Saks and Macy's, two of the city's leading department stores, had bought property on Thirty-fourth Street and Broadway, breaking away from "The Ladies' Mile," a stretch of stores that had Twenty-third Street as its northern boundary. People began speaking of Thirty-fourth Street as the new retail center of the city. Added to this, after Cassatt's plans for his new station hit the newspapers, speculators began buying up parcels of land along Thirty-fourth Street as far west as Eighth Avenue.

Nevertheless, questions still remained. Would other retail stores follow Macy's and Saks, and would the spillover reach Pennsylvania Station? Or would the blocks of tenements and saloons cut off the station from the rest of the city?

On May 10, 1903, the *New York Herald* was very sanguine about the effect the new Pennsylvania Station would have on the neighborhood:

> With the advent of the Pennsylvania's big station and tunnel in the heart of the old Tenderloin, that famous landmark of vice and blackmail passes into history. . . . Smart shops and resplendent bazaars will line the new streets and plazas of the old Tenderloin site. Here, the wealth and fashion of the metropolis will mingle with crowds from the country, thronging the grand corridors of the palace station, to be whisked between town and country under the floods of Hell Gate and the Hudson with magic speed and luxury.

Thirty years before, Cornelius Vanderbilt had built his station at the end of the world. Now it was the hub around which other buildings grew. Cassatt could only look at the land on which his station would rise and wonder: would history repeat itself, or would Pennsylvania Station be known as a palace in Hell's Kitchen?

In 1902 the R. H. Macy Company opened its new department store in Herald Square. The small building at the left of the huge Palladian structure is a nondescript house bought for the then stunning price of $375,000 by an old rival of Macy's who held onto the eyesore out of pure spite. In the early years of the century the trains of the Sixth Avenue elevated, in the foreground, were still pulled by sturdy little steam locomotives.

During the early stages of the work on the station, railroad tracks from the Hudson River tunnels replaced Thirty-second Street and ran on a temporary trestle into the center of the excavation.

CHAPTER SEVEN

"I CAN SEE
DOWN TO CHINA!"

There was nothing remarkable about the building. It was a tenement standing on the north side of Thirty-second Street on the edge of Eleventh Avenue. If one cared to trace its history, number 557 would probably reveal itself to have been built sometime after staid, prosperous Chelsea had succumbed to the poverty of its northern neighbor, Hell's Kitchen. Or perhaps, sitting on a tenuous border, it may once have been the home of a middle-class family, only to find its rooms divided and crowded with the poor.

On the morning of February 25, 1903, four months before work on the tunnel shafts had begun, number 557 was torn down. The event drew dignitaries from the Pennsylvania Railroad, who posed in front of the building's shabby entrance while the house-wrecking crew stood on several of its fire escapes. Among the eminent were Charles Jacobs, chief engineer for the North River Division of the tunneling project; Alfred Noble, head of the railroad's East River tunnels; and Gustav Lindenthal, the architect whose Hudson River bridge would never be built. (Lindenthal would resign from the Pennsylvania Railroad on December 15, 1903, and go on in 1909 to build New York's Queensborough Bridge, connecting Manhattan with Queens, and, later, the New York Connecting Bridge, over Hell Gate, for the Pennsylvania.)

The occasion was momentous for the Pennsylvania Railroad: number 557 was the first building to be demolished for the tunnel. Before work was completed five hundred buildings would be razed and more than fifteen hundred people displaced. Entire blocks of tenements, shops, factories, and eventually a Catholic church would be leveled for the tunnels coming into the new station from under the Hudson.

During the process of excavation, Thirty-second Street became a trestle road leading to a scow dump on the site of the demolished tenement. The dump held all the sand and stone taken from the excavation site. Eventually Thirty-second Street would disappear entirely, to be replaced by the network of tracks feeding into the new station.

In the spring of 1904, a year after number 557 was demolished, a classic battle of property owner versus builder erupted when the railroad attempted to condemn the rest of the property on Thirty-second Street between Ninth and Tenth avenues. Several owners, seeing an opportunity to get rich quick, demanded compensation that bordered on extortion. Others, simply not wanting to let go, tried to convince the courts that their property should not be leveled, no matter what the railroad offered them.

The railroad had already committed itself to rebuilding a church that stood on Ninth Avenue between Thirty-first and Thirty-second streets. In exchange for the land on which Saint Michael's Church stood, the railroad purchased another site for the church on the south side of Thirty-fourth Street between Ninth and Tenth avenues and had the church meticulously rebuilt, complete with rectory, convent, and school. Every stone from the original facade was numbered, removed, and reassembled at the new location. The magnificent marble altar was also rebuilt for the new church. The project was said to cost the Pennsylvania Railroad close to one million dollars.

Fortunately for the railroad, several years before Cassatt announced plans to build the station he had had the foresight to instruct Stuyvesant Real Estate Company, acting on the railroad's behalf, quietly to acquire most of the other property needed. Considering that the building of Pennsylvania Station and the clearing of land for its track area would raze six city blocks, a successful campaign on the part of other property owners could have held up construction for years and added tremendously to its already heavy cost.

Not only did Cassatt have to buy the blocks of houses and factories on which his station would stand, he had to obtain permission to tunnel under property all the way from the station's Seventh Avenue entrance to the edge of the East River.

The permission rarely came cheaply. John Radley, whose iron foundry was located on Thirty-fourth Street east of Fifth Avenue, was offered $400 by the railroad for the right to tunnel under his property. Radley balked at this small sum and took his case to the New York State Supreme Court, where Justice Gildersleeve ordered the Pennsylvania Railroad to pay a startling $24,750. As a result of Radley's settlement, the railroad was forced to pay other property owners similar amounts.

Almost a year after the Radley ruling, the railroad was still buying property, but no longer in run-down neighborhoods. On April 12, 1905, a small stir followed the discovery that the Pennsylvania had bought two town houses, numbers 43 and 45, on East Thirty-third Street, close to Park Avenue and midway between the site of the station on Seventh Avenue and the tunnel workings at the foot of East Thirty-second and Thirty-third streets. People began to wonder if plans were more ambitious than had originally been stated. Did the railroad intend to build an exit from their tunnels on the East Side of Manhattan? As it turned out, these town houses would be demolished to make way for a shaft from which tunnel work could be carried out in two directions.

Several months after the town house purchases, the Pennsylvania bought more property east of Seventh Avenue. The extent of Cassatt's project was not fully appreciated until New Yorkers began to see the amount of property he had to acquire. Not only was the railroad building a monumental station that would occupy several city blocks, it was tunneling under the streets of Manhattan from one side of the island to the other. Even Cassatt did not know just how complicated that tunneling would become as his engineers had to skirt gas lines, sewers, and building foundations.

In the area where the station would rise, demolition crews were busy razing all the buildings Cassatt had purchased. By the time they were finished, in August 1907, five million bricks and six thousand truckloads of timber, iron fixtures, and miscellaneous bits and pieces had been carted down the trestle road to the scow dump.

The excavation for the new station was incredible to see. The hole went down fifty-eight feet through New York gneiss. It stretched for two city blocks on either side of Eighth Avenue, which, now nothing more than a narrow bridge, had been closed to traffic. Realizing that most New Yorkers were curious about the site, the *New York Herald* sent one of its reporters to the great hole, as it was known, and on October 29, 1905, printed what he saw:

> The appearance of the busiest sections of the Panama Canal is reproduced in realistic fashion within a block of Broadway. The immense tract bounded by Seventh and Ninth avenues and Thirty-first and Thirty-second streets today is a very anthill of activity. As quickly as the buildings disappeared from this once closely populated district an immense amount of excavating machinery was installed. Railroad tracks were laid in every direction and the ground soon lost all semblance of its former civilization. To-day the resemblance to the canal zone is complete. The land once reduced to the dead level of stone pavements and asphalted streets has been ridged and furrowed until its original topography is but a memory. Long, uneven alleys stretch east and west upward of half a mile in length, through which noisy trains pass on a very busy schedule. The depth of these valleys at many points completely hides the trains from the surrounding country. At several points the tract is dominated by several hills which rise twenty feet or more above the level of the valleys. There are several miles of railroad tracks in constant use, with switches and crossings—a complete railroad system.

The railroad tracks ran down the trestle road where battered flatcars heaped with rock and earth made their way to the scow dump. It was at Tenth Avenue and Thirty-second Street, standing above the portals of the tunnels coming in from under the Hudson River, that one could really see the immensity of the Pennsylvania's invasion of New York. Looking eastward from this elevation, one saw a huge channel sliced through the rock, resembling the Culebra Cut, made for the Panama Canal. But here, instead of tropical jungle surrounding the quarry, there was the melancholy line of tenements, their network of washlines exposed to the crowds who came to gape.

Working around Ninth Avenue proved to be a very tricky business for the railroad. Not only was there the problem of added traffic caused by the closing of Eighth Avenue, there was also the problem of the Ninth Avenue el. An elaborate system of beams and support posts was devised—at the railroad's expense—to absorb the constant rattle of construction that might derail trains as they made their way overhead past the excavation. No blasting was done near the supports while trains were passing over, although trains had to be stopped sometimes when a heavy blasting period was in progress. The work of digging a foundation for the new railroad was extremely difficult, particularly since sewers and water and gas mains had to be protected from drills, derricks, and dislodged rock. A single accident could

Above: As the excavation proceeded, increasing care had to be taken to keep nearby gas and water mains from rupturing and to ensure that the supports for the Ninth Avenue elevated were not weakened.

Right: Far from the site of the new station, a shaft for the Pennsylvania's East River tunnels intrudes into a quiet neighborhood on East Thirty-second Street.

affect an entire neighborhood. Watchmen were kept on duty day and night to make sure no mishaps occurred.

It was no wonder that people looked down in awe at this multilevel excavation, which exposed parts of Manhattan never seen before. Down in the hole there was another city: it mesmerized onlookers. Amid the ever-present din of the drills that perched, like monstrous birds, on nearly inaccessible places as they reduced boulders to so many rocks, Lilliputian men commanded derricks to lift the dislodged rubble onto cars. Other men supervised the bracing of wooden forms against the sides of the excavation where concrete would be poured to form permanent retaining walls. The daily lineup of bowler hats peering down at the activity became a source of amusement to the workmen below. "I can see down to China!" was soon a cliché.

But what of the building that would rise from this quarry? In early 1906 small items began to appear in the *New York Times* describing how the station would look. The Doric monument would encompass six city blocks, said the *Times*, and its total size would be that of a football field. There were also the inevitable comparisons with existing railroad stations. Pennsylvania Station would be nearly twice as big as the Hamburg terminal, which was then the world's largest, and almost three times the size of the South Station in Boston or the Saint Louis Terminal, the two biggest stations in the United States.

The allusion to size was tantalizing. But as yet there had been no pictures, and the public did not know what to expect. Finally, on May 20, 1906, the first sketch of the new station appeared in the *New York Times*.

On a spring day in 1907 passersby pause at the corner of Thirty-third Street and Eighth Avenue to watch the digging and blasting.

CHAPTER EIGHT

SHADOWS OVER THE GREAT STATION

Those New Yorkers who were old enough and lucky enough to walk through the city's Crystal Palace during its three-year life before fire destroyed it in 1856 must have been astonished when they opened their *Times* that spring morning. Before them was an apparition, a steel-and-glass reincarnation of the famous exhibition hall that once stood on Forty-second Street and Sixth Avenue, a block west of the Croton Reservoir. Like its London counterpart, which had been built for the Great Exhibition of 1851, New York's Crystal Palace was inspired by the conservatories and train sheds of Europe. Its delicate iron frame gave American architects an idea of the metal's versatility, allowing them to reach beyond the limitations imposed by brick and stone.

The exterior of Pennsylvania Station was impressive enough, with its two-block row of Doric columns rising to the sleek, flat roof. But what made one's heart leap was the interior: the artist's rendering of the concourse, with its exposed floor opening onto the tracks and its great domed roof. The pen-and-ink drawing showed a mass of treillage arches rising in dramatic sweeps. Yet like the Crystal Palace, this train shed, with its awesome space that bespoke power and strength, managed also to convey the charm and lightness of a Victorian gazebo.

For Charles McKim it must have been an emotional moment when his creation was uncoupled from his vision and given over to the people for whom it would be built. The man who had stood before the Baths of Caracalla on a June afternoon five years earlier now anxiously watched the public's reaction to his new railroad station.

McKim had to argue with the Pennsylvania Railroad to preserve the integrity of his design. The Pennsylvania's board of directors liked the work well enough, but they wanted to use the valuable air space above the station for building a hotel. McKim was firm. He told the board of directors that the Pennsylvania Railroad owed the city of New York a monumental gateway, a building whose sole purpose was the arrival and departure of trains. The board argued that they were spending an enormous amount of money to tunnel under two rivers and across the breadth of Manhattan; the materials for the new station would be the finest marble, the best iron, the most beautiful wood, all crafted by design engineers who would spare no cost to

When the walls of the station began to rise, New Yorkers finally got some inkling of what the finished building would look like.

With its delicate traceries of iron supporting acres of glass, New York City's short-lived Crystal Palace prefigured McKim's grand steel-and-glass concourse.

achieve the effect McKim was after. Could the railroad not have this one concession—a hotel? McKim exercised all of his power of persuasion to convince the board to let his design stand unaltered. One might as well have put a hotel above the Baths of Caracalla. William A. Boring, who worked with McKim, later said, "To Mr. McKim the question of beauty was not confined to architecture. He saw beauty wherever it was; and he insisted that things accessory to architecture and to life in general should conform to his ideal of good taste." Beauty was a philosophy, a way of life.

McKim was fortunate. Alexander Cassatt understood exactly how he felt. Beauty, after all, was his philosophy as well. Had he not carried with him his own vision of the Baths of Caracalla? After initially siding with his board of directors Cassatt agreed with McKim that his railroad should celebrate its arrival into the country's first city with a building as grand and as beautiful as could be conceived.

It was a time of glory for McKim. Now the building that began as a flicker of artistic vision was rising just eleven blocks north of his offices. Excitement had been escalating steadily as the mammoth structure began to take form. Already people were saying that Pennsylvania Station might

82

prove to be the architect's best work. But for McKim the days of basking in accomplishment were numbered. The fifty-nine-year-old architect had been feeling ill for a while, and by 1906 he was spending very few days in the offices on Twenty-first Street and Fifth Avenue. By the time the sketches of his station appeared in the *New York Times* McKim had chosen William Symmes Richardson, one of the firm's younger architects and a new partner, to finish his work. Although McKim had established the basic design, it was Richardson who executed the details.

There was another shadow—so tragic and futile that it would alter the way Charles McKim faced his remaining years. On June 24, 1906, one month after the station drawings had appeared in the newspapers, McKim's partner and lifelong friend, Stanford White, was shot by a man named Harry Thaw. Heir to forty million dollars in Pennsylvania Railroad bonds, Thaw was a drug-addicted sadist who harbored a festering jealousy of Stanford White. Evelyn Nesbitt, Thaw's wife, had been White's child-mistress, and to Thaw's tormented mind the architect had enslaved her. White had robbed Evelyn—or, more precisely, had robbed Harry Thaw—of her virtue.

If McKim was devastated by the loss of his friend, the manner of his death must have tortured him all the more. On the day of his murder White had been busy with the final details of the Madison Square Presbyterian Church, which he had begun in 1903 for the Reverend Charles H. Parkhurst, the preacher who had worked so vigorously to rid the Tenderloin of its unsavory characters. The church White designed, with its glazed terra-cotta walls and green granite columns, glowed with color—raising a storm of protest, according to White's biographer, Charles C. Baldwin, "as being barbaric, pagan, a thing of beauty rather than a house of prayer."

The idea of disparaging something because it is beautiful must have made White laugh. Never one to bow to the philistines White spent this evening on the roof garden of another building he had designed, one whose magnificent tower, modeled after the Giralda Tower of Seville Cathedral, was topped by Augustus Saint-Gaudens's controversial nude Diana. In Madison Square Garden's tower, heavily curtained against daylight, "Stanny" White threw his famous parties for those fortunate enough to be part of his inner circle. It was also here that he and the sixteen-year-old Evelyn Nesbitt would linger long after the guests had left. They would climb the spiral stairs to the top, where Evelyn, clinging to the heel of Diana—the statue supposedly done in her likeness—would look out over Manhattan and watch the dawn rising over the East River.

White's Madison Square Garden was built on the site of the old New York and Harlem Railroad station, before the railroad had been forced by the city's Common Council to move uptown and build Grand Central Depot. Ironically, White's Madison Square Garden itself would be destroyed in 1925, to be reincarnated that same year at Eighth Avenue between Forty-ninth and Fiftieth streets. Later a third Madison Square Garden would rise, but this time over the ruins of Charles McKim's Pennsylvania Station.

Upon White's death, the papers made much of his affairs with young women in general and of Evelyn Nesbitt in particular. But little was said of the greatness of the architect, the man whose talents would one day be compared to Cellini's and whose buildings would grace New York City for

The public got its first glimpse of the station's vast interior spaces when the McKim, Mead and White drawings appeared in the New York Times *on May 20, 1906. Above are the concourse and tracks. The main waiting room is at top right, and the arcade opposite.*

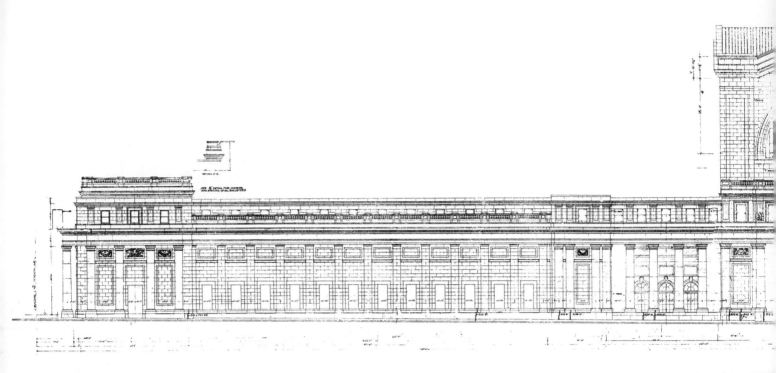

NEW YORK TERM
THIRT

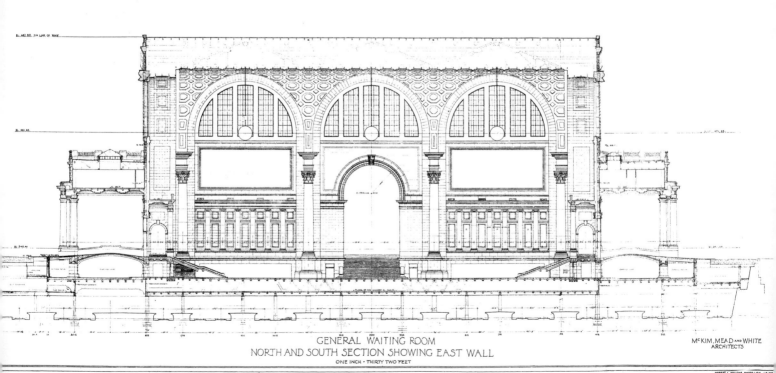

GENERAL WAITING ROOM
NORTH AND SOUTH SECTION SHOWING EAST WALL
ONE INCH · THIRTY TWO FEET

McKIM, MEAD AND WHITE
ARCHITECTS

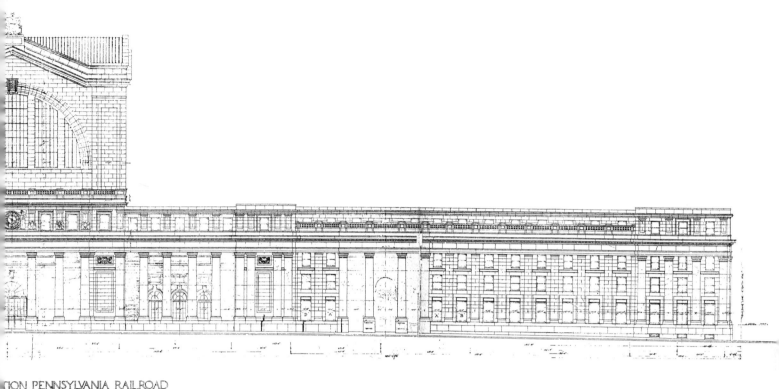

TION PENNSYLVANIA RAILROAD
STREET ELEVATION
THIRTY TWO FEET

McKIM, MEAD AND WHITE
ARCHITECTS

many years to come. Such recognition came later, after too many of his works had been destroyed.

The shadow that was cast over McKim's life reached beyond him and to his project. On the day the account of the murder ran in the *New York Times*, another article appeared. It, too, was front-page news. The headline said nearly everything: WORK STOPPED ON PENNSYLVANIA TUNNELS.

All the tunneling east of the new Pennsylvania Station was part of the railroad's East River Division, headed by Alfred Noble. The work was in turn subdivided into three segments, each different from the others. The crosstown tunnels, those running from Seventh to First avenues under Manhattan to the East River portals, comprised the first segment. These tunnels were being dug almost exclusively through Manhattan schist, the same rock encountered in tunneling from the banks of the Hudson to the new station. On the Queens side, the tunnels rose to the surface from under the East River through ground that was little more than a tidal flat along Newtown Creek. Unlike the Hudson River tunnels through Bergen Hill, in New Jersey, these faced no mountain of hard rock to be bored through. An open-trench method was used on this segment, since there would be no need to cover the tunnels.

The tunnels running underneath the East River, the third segment, would consist of four tubes, linking up with the crosstown tunnels on the Manhattan side and the Long Island City tunnels on the other. It was here, beneath

Less evocative but more detailed than the renderings in the Times, *these elevations served as working drawings. The east wall of the main waiting room shows the Grand Stairway leading to the arcade.*

87

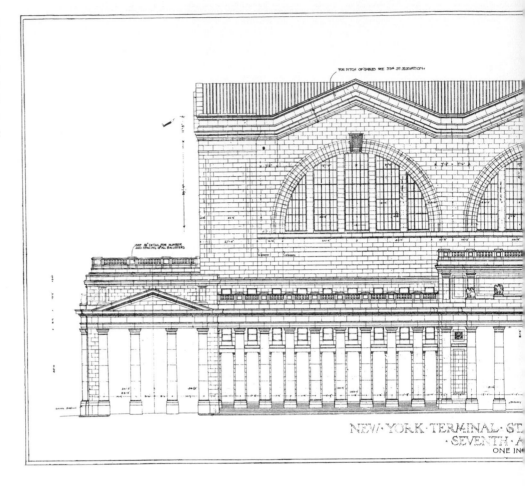

treacherous currents, that the trouble began. From the outset, the engineers had known that the bed of the East River, which began on the Manhattan side as gravel and boulders and then became the solid rock that was the top of a glacial ridge, would present immense problems. At times the tunnels had to go through the gravel and then through the hard glacial ridge, and parts of the tunnels had soft gravel above and hard glacial ridge below.

Throughout the spring there had been reports of leaks in the East River tunnels. Passengers on the Thirty-fourth Street ferry reported seeing violent commotions in the river near the Long Island City ferry slips. A miniature geyser, evidently caused by a blowout, sprayed mist over the startled passengers.

Then, on June 20, 1906, at six-fifteen in the morning, workers at the Thirty-fourth Street ferry house heard a roar coming from the East River. A column of water thirty, perhaps forty, feet high, exploded into the air. Water around the geyser boiled as the men at the ferry house looked on in amazement. Eighty-six feet below, twenty men trapped in the flooding tunnel desperately scrambled for safety. When it was over, two were injured and two others were dead. The bodies were still lying undiscovered somewhere in the riverbed when a coroner's jury, impounded to decide the case against the contractors for previous deaths attributed to the bends, voted to censure the contractors severely.

Seven days after the tragedy Alexander Cassatt came to New York with Samuel Rea to talk with the engineers in charge of the East River tunnels.

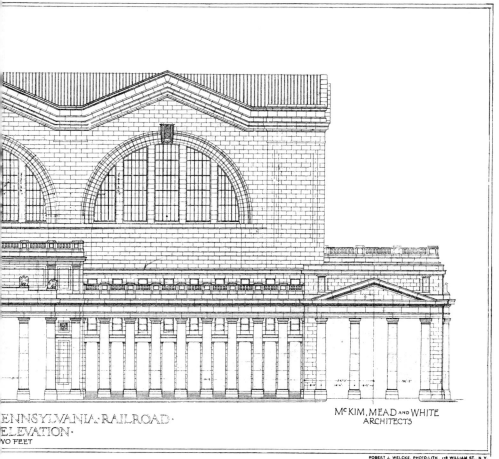

ENNSYLVANIA⋅RAILROAD⋅
ELEVATION⋅
VO FEET

McKIM,MEAD AND WHITE⋅
ARCHITECTS

Charles Jacobs, Cassatt's chief engineer, was in Europe, said to be studying the latest methods of tunneling under large bodies of water. Delays caused by strikes, trouble with air pressure, and the inexperience of some of the workers had multiplied building costs. Rumors circulating among the city's engineering community that the East River tunnels would not be finished for six years reached the press and were reported by the *New York Times* on June 28. Two days later Samuel Rea, in an interview with a *New York Times* reporter, defended the practices of S. Pearson & Son, the English contractors responsible for the East River tunnels. He explained the problems—some foreseen and others unexpected—of digging under the East River.

The delays, the rising costs, the strikes, all were problems that weighed on Alexander Cassatt, but none so heavily as the loss of life. It was the one thing he wanted to avoid, the one cost he was not prepared to bear.

The sixty-six-year-old president of the Pennsylvania Railroad was tired, dispirited. As early as 1894 doctors had warned Lois Cassatt, his wife, that heart disease might kill him at any time.

As if the tunnel disaster and ill health were not burden enough, Cassatt had to live with a family tragedy he could never quite accept. On April 11, 1905, his favorite daughter, Katherine, newly married, barely thirty-three, died of complications due to goiter, a condition whose cure was discovered just months after her death. Later Lois Cassatt would write to one of her children, "Her loss to us and her husband was irreparable, and

89

I feel now that your father was never able to get over the shock of her death."

A few days after Samuel Rea met the press to defend the East River tunnel contractors, Alexander Cassatt accompanied his family on a much-needed vaction to Four Acres, their new summer home in Bar Harbor, Maine. No sooner had the family settled in than one of the Cassatt grand-children came down with whooping cough. The virulent and at that time dreaded disease spread quickly among all the children, and instead of resting, Cassatt, himself suffering from the illness, spent most of his days nursing the children back to health.

While Cassatt tried to recuperate in Maine, the date had been set for joining the two sections of the north tunnel under the Hudson. The event was due to occur on September 18, but first, measurements had to be checked and double-checked to make sure that the two sections of the tunnel would indeed meet. Unlike the seemingly plagued East River tunnels those under the Hudson had encountered few problems, and the engineers were optimistic. Still, tension mounted as September 18 approached.

At midnight on Saturday, September 2, all work under the Hudson River was stopped for a last-minute check on measurements. Three years had passed since the first gang of sandhogs descended into the shafts on either side of the Hudson, pushing their shields toward the river's center where, finally, the crews would meet. But despite all the planning and calculation, no one could say, until the final moment, whether the engineers had succeeded or failed.

Sometime before September 18, a group of sandhogs decided to make their own test and hold their own celebration. Several men working in the New York end of the tube brought a box of cigars into the tunnel and passed it through a small hole to their New Jersey colleagues. A few days later, the engineers confirmed what the sandhogs already knew: the two shields aligned perfectly. For the next several days work continued in an atmosphere of expectation, until, on September 12, six days ahead of schedule, the shields met, coming together rim to rim, like two gargantuan tumblers. The first of the Pennsylvania's tunnels was complete.

Alexander Cassatt was supposed to be the first person to ride a tram car through the tunnel when it was finally finished, but there is no record that he was able to make the trip. His health, already fragile, was further taxed by whooping cough. In any case it was the joining of the second river tube, on October 9, that got the publicity and gave readers of the *New York Times* a sense of what it was like inside a tunnel ninety-five feet below the Hudson's surface:

> Early yesterday morning a party of thirty workmen, commonly called "sandhogs," who had gone down the Manhattan shaft several hours before, heard shouts coming from beyond the big circular shield in motion before them. The shield machinery . . . was stopped, and a man with a pick crawled into the trap on one side and began digging away at the soft mud. It was not very long before the point of a pick came through from the other side, and in a few seconds there was a hole big enough to see through.

On the other side of the hole the man with the pick saw thirty sandhogs from Weehawken staring back at him. History was made by a group of grime-covered men, some of whom barely spoke English. They walked beneath the Hudson River, from New Jersey to Manhattan, and back again by the north tunnel, the one completed in September.

October 9, 1906, was a day of celebration. In the afternoon reporters were invited to tour the tunnel, and by evening Charles Jacobs, George Gibbs, Alfred Noble, and all the engineers who had helped Cassatt build his tunnels took the same walk beneath the river. The arched sides of the tubes were strung with incandescent lights. It was hazy and cold inside, and the pressurized air, so unnatural, made one uneasy. The iron rings that formed the tunnel were all linked together now and the muddy wooden planks beneath the men's feet were covered with sawdust.

Muck and mud and rust were everywhere. They reminded the men of how short a time had passed since the sandhogs had worked their shifts to keep the riverbed from invading the tunnels. When the engineers and press corps got to the spot where the headings had finally come together, just west of the New York state line, Charles Jacobs proudly showed the reporters that the shields had not been misaligned by so much as a single inch. When the submarine pedestrians had walked their way to Weehawken, they exited the south tube and entered the north, completed nearly a month before. At the point in the north tube where the headings joined, an American flag fashioned of red, white, and blue light bulbs greeted the party. There were speeches and congratulations and a final three-cheer salute to President Cassatt.

But work in the tunnels was far from over. Massive columns had to be sunk every fifteen feet into bedrock beneath the belly of the tubes to sustain the weight of the trains that would pass through. Concrete two feet thick would line each tube, and a platform had to be built along the walls, the entire length of the tunnels. Engineers estimated that another year and a half would pass before trains could run in the Hudson River tunnels.

Despite the immense success of the Hudson tubes, bad luck continued to plague the East River tunnels. At seven o'clock on the evening of December 3, the premature explosion of forty pounds of dynamite in one of the tubes near Long Island City instantly killed three men and injured a dozen more, two of whom died the following day.

The new deaths bore down cruelly upon Cassatt. They came, too, at a time when he had been badly shaken by revelations made during a recent Interstate Commerce Commission coal inquiry that officials of his railroad, men he knew and trusted, had accepted graft. The blow was especially bitter to a man who once stood fast and prevailed against New York legislators who demanded bribes to allow his station to come into New York City.

By early December, Cassatt no longer went to his offices on Broad Street. Lois Cassatt tried to keep the house quiet so her husband could get some desperately needed rest. But the quiet did not help. For the first time since they were married, Lois canceled the family Christmas dinner. The household tried to go about the business of their lives, to avoid looking as though they were on deathwatch, but it was impossible for them to hide the sense of what was happening.

On December 28, 1906, at one o'clock in the afternoon, the president of the Pennsylvania Railroad died in his home on Rittenhouse Square, Philadelphia. He was just twenty days into his sixty-seventh year.

CHAPTER NINE

A SEASON OF MISFORTUNE

It was the first spring since Cassatt's death. The misfortunes that had hastened his passing haunted the tunnels and the new terminal. People still came to gape into the enormous crater between Thirty-first and Thirty-third streets, but now their curiosity was tinged with apprehension.

The past several months had given them cause to wonder just how safe all this excavating was. The first sign of trouble came in February, when the back wheels of a coal wagon traveling along Thirty-third Street near the Waldorf-Astoria suddenly gave way. The ground beneath the wheels caved in, leaving the coal wagon half buried. It was apparent to onlookers that the tunneling had weakened the streets to the point of collapse.

Until the collapse the sandhogs had been boring through the Manhattan schist with great success. On January 4, 1907, a month before the coal wagon accident, they had celebrated a minor victory when the headings below one of the crosstown streets came together. An Italian foreman, determined to make history, worked at the tunnel twenty-four hours straight so he could be the first to reach the connection that made clear passage from Fifth Avenue to the East River.

There was just one more segment of tunnel to go, between Fifth Avenue and the entry to the new terminal at Seventh Avenue, and the work would be finished. But as the sandhogs continued to drive westward from Fifth Avenue they found themselves standing in sand and water. Then the water gushed down on them, forcing all work to a halt. The engineers of the United Engineering and Contracting Company, who were boring the tunnels, checked a topographical map made in 1865. It showed a stream flowing east from Sixth Avenue and Thirty-third Street into a pond that ended at Kip's Bay. Apparently, the remnants of that stream still flowed beneath the street. The mishap with the coal wagon confirmed their suspicions: the sandhogs were no longer boring through hard, predictable rock, but through water and quicksand.

They would have to use the "cut and cover" method of tunneling now, which meant tearing open Thirty-second and Thirty-third streets from Fifth Avenue to Seventh and replacing them with wooden roadways. It also meant that for approximately ten months people who lived in the town houses and apartment buildings in the area would have to live not only with the

Onlookers were present throughout every stage of construction. This particular batch is taking it all in on April 29, 1907.

93

inconvenience of torn-up pavement and wooden roadways but with the fear that, like the coal wagon, their homes would sink into the tunnels.

For weeks merchants and property owners locked horns with the United Engineering and Contracting Company. The contractors needed a permit to open the streets, and the people who lived and worked in the area wanted them to find an alternative. But there was none, the contractors insisted. The tunnel work remained at a standstill until in mid-February the Rapid Transit Commission granted the permit and the streets were opened.

Now it was May 25—eleven-thirty on a Sunday morning. Sightseers were lined up in their usual places along the edges of the station excavation site. Seventh Avenue was jammed with trucks and wagons. The sidewalks were crowded with Sunday shoppers who stopped now and again to look into the great pit or to chat with one another about the inconvenience of getting around all this construction.

Isaac Finesilver and Jacob Kosty, owners of a secondhand clothing store, were talking on the street in front of their shop. Mrs. Finesilver had just invited Mr. and Mrs. Kosty to dinner with their new baby. Suddenly an explosion—an erupting volcano—tore through the air. Mrs. Kosty reeled as an avalanche of rocks cascaded through the dining room wall, knocking down a chandelier. Fragments ricocheted about the room.

A block away, on Thirty-first Street, a Mrs. Melonius was on her roof hanging her wash when a stone struck her back and knocked her down. There was pandemonium in the streets as people ran from the boulders, some weighing several hundred pounds, that tore through the air like artillery shells. For several minutes a blizzard of dust blinded everyone left in the streets. When the storm was over, twelve people had been injured, some severely. Windows were shattered for blocks around, and nearby stores were so pummeled that it was difficult to determine what they had been selling.

After the dust had settled it was discovered that a charge of dynamite placed next to a rock in a pit near the corner of Seventh Avenue and Thirty-fourth Street had failed to go off several days before. No one had noticed the unexploded charge, but on this Sunday morning something had triggered it. Scenes like this led some people to suspect that the gods of progress frowned upon the tunnel and terminal project.

Meanwhile other tunnels under the Hudson and East rivers were being completed. In December 1906, the time of Cassatt's death, Brooklyn and Manhattan were linked by tunnel when the first underwater subway, from the Battery in lower Manhattan to the shores of Brooklyn, was completed. Now commuters could reach Manhattan not only by the Brooklyn Bridge and the Brooklyn Ferry but by the subway as well. The long-awaited McAdoo tunnels connecting New Jersey with New York were making steady progress as well. In February 1907 the *New York Times* heralded the achievement in a lengthy article promising that by September two miles of the tunnel would be opened to the public.

For the Pennsylvania Railroad, however, progress was painfully slow, and success seemed to move further and further into the future. The months dragged on from spring into summer, and then came another accident. On July 2, as one hundred and fifty workmen walked through one of the tunnels, a huge boulder escaped from its fastenings, crushing two men to death and injuring many more. Despite this most recent tragedy, tunneling and excavating continued into the winter without incident. But as the New Year arrived, there was one final note of sadness.

On New Year's Day, 1908, Charles McKim returned from a hunting trip in South Carolina. No one remembered seeing much of him after that. Ever since the death of his friend and partner White, McKim's spirits had been low. Possibly to escape his melancholia, he accepted a burdensome amount of work. A month later rumors began to circulate that the sixty-one-year-old architect was suffering from shattered nerves and heart problems. Neither his firm nor his daughter, Margaret, would comment, but it appeared certain that Charles McKim was in a private sanitarium not far from New York.

That same month, however, a little more than a year after Cassatt's death, the gods seemed finally appeased. On January 13 the tunnel bores connecting Long Island City with the East River were completed. Because of past accidents caused by blowouts in the soft material of the riverbed, the engineers decided that the shields for all four tunnels should meet where the riverbed was solid rock. The shields from Manhattan reached the selected place first, and tunnel driving was stopped on that side while the crew waited for the sandhogs from Long Island.

While they waited, a bulkhead of concrete and sandbags was built at the cutting edges of each shield, closing the shield faces. This ensured the sandhogs' safety: air pressure in the approaching tunnel headings would be different, and as the thickness of the dividing wall was decreased, there was danger of it being blown out. There was also an atmosphere of competition among the work gangs (each wanted its heading to be the first connected), and sealing the faces of the shields the engineers made certain that overzealous workmen would not be tempted to open them prematurely.

While the bulkhead was being built, eight-inch steel pipes were forced forward for approximately fifty feet toward the Long Island side to check the alignment before the shields actually met. As soon as the Long Island shields reached the end of the pipes, the workmen discovered that they could speak with their brothers on the Manhattan side; in fact, the strong air current flowing through the pipes even let them send objects from one end to the other. The men in D tunnel, the first to meet its Manhattan mate, placed a toy train in the pipe—the first "train" to pass through the tunnel. Later when the men in B tunnel sent a rag doll through their pipe, it became the first "lady" to make the trip and was presented as a souvenir to the engineers in charge of the tunnel.

Finally it came time for the shields to meet. Tunnel officials had planned to make the first entrance through a wooden door installed for this purpose when the bulkhead between the tunnel headings had been made. It was kept securely locked, but a day before the official opening, eager sandhogs began tearing at the concrete bulkhead until they had made a hole big enough for a man to squeeze through. Then they held their own celebration. The body of water that had been for some of their comrades a river of death was finally conquered.

CHAPTER TEN

THE LIGHT AT THE END

Daylight shines into an East River tunnel. Now the track must be laid, and the walls lined with concrete.

A little after seven o'clock on a Saturday morning in April 1908, a group of engineers picked their way over piles of broken stone and dirt under Bergen Hill, in New Jersey, until they came upon a wall of rock. It was a final, thin layer of stone that separated them from another tunnel that had been pushed through from the Hackensack Meadows. Into the thin ledge a boring was made to prepare for a dynamite blast.

At exactly 7:05, the blast went off. As the smoke began to clear, a glimmer of light penetrated the darkness. The traprock of Bergen Hill was the most stubborn material the engineers had encountered in all of the tunnel work. It had taken an average of three pounds of dynamite for every cubic yard of rock removed. Another blast was set off. This time, there was an opening large enough for the engineers to make their way through. It was now possible to walk through Bergen Hill, under the Hudson River, under the island of Manhattan, and under the East River, finally to exit at Long Island City.

A month later, on May 7, the final heading of the second Hudson River tube—the last of all the headings and tunnels the Pennsylvania Railroad had driven—was blown away by a final blast of dynamite. Sixteen miles of tunnel had been dug, and three million cubic yards of rock and earth scooped out.

That night, Charles Jacobs, Cassatt's chief engineer, took his staff to Sherry's Restaurant to celebrate. The sense that the worst was over was apparent on their faces: the cloud that had hung over the project for so long was finally beginning to lift.

Within the next few months, all of the tubes would be concreted and cleaned out in readiness for the laying of roadbed and track and the installation of the electrical equipment necessary to run the trains. By summer a corps of Pennsylvania Railroad engineers would spend a day studying the electrical system of the New York Central so they could determine what would be needed for the new Pennsylvania Railroad tunnels and terminal.

George Westinghouse was told in November 1908 that his firm had been awarded the contract to electrify the new Pennsylvania tunnels. It was no surprise. Westinghouse had already built a huge electric locomotive for tests, and the engine had been operating night and day over a special track

A 1909 postcard of a traditional New York harbor scene found space to celebrate the newly completed Hudson tunnels.

on the Long Island. Westinghouse had been a close friend to Cassatt, who
had intended all along to put him in charge of the electrification.

By 1908, it was clear that Manhattan had entered a new era in transportation.
On February 25, three months before the sandhogs blasted away the last
heading in the Hudson River tubes, service through another tunnel under
the Hudson was inaugurated. At three-thirty that afternoon, Theodore Roosevelt, now president of the United States, pressed a button in the White
House that sent a current of electricity two hundred and fifty miles northward
to a train waiting at a station on Nineteenth Street and Sixth Avenue in
New York. The cars lighted up, and the motors began to turn. Two minutes
later William McAdoo sounded a bell, and the train started to move. Eight
hundred people who were crammed into the cars gave a resounding cheer
as the train moved slowly down Sixth Avenue, turning at Morton Street,
where it descended under the Hudson. Eleven minutes later William McAdoo
stepped onto the platform and shouted to the rest of the passengers, "Hoboken!
All out!"

The age of the commuter had truly arrived. Not only would the Battery
Tunnel provide quick and frequent service to Brooklyn, the McAdoo tunnels
would bring New Jersey residents to Manhattan. And before very long trains
of the Long Island Railroad would descend beneath the East River, delivering
commuters to Pennsylvania Station. There was also a plan, encouraged by
the Pennsylvania Railroad, to bring New York's subway system to the new
station.

Less than ten years after Cassatt had decided to take his railroad into
Manhattan, the old, brownstone city of the nineteenth century was quickly
vanishing. Even Grand Central Station was changing. Barely a decade had
passed since the depot had undergone major renovation and had been given
a new name. Now Vanderbilt's railroad terminus was scheduled to be
remodeled once more. This time, the burgeoning railroad and commuter
traffic demanded a whole new station. Electrification of the tracks meant
that the land north of the station could be covered over and built upon,
transforming the character of the streets from wooden homes and factories
to the elegant town houses and apartment buildings of Park Avenue. In
1903 several architectural firms, including that of McKim, Mead and White,
were invited to submit designs for the new terminal. Two firms, Warren
and Wetmore, and Reed & Stem, were awarded the unusual and complicated
task of collaborating on the new building. The result was a beaux-arts
structure christened Grand Central Terminal.

By February 1909 another station was beginning to take form, and New
Yorkers had their first glimpse of the building they had been anticipating
for nearly a decade. It was rising like an ancient temple from an earthen
tomb, the first of its four granite facades extending more than 430 feet
along Seventh Avenue. The pink Milford stone was startlingly pristine amid
the construction rubble.

Facing the structure from Thirty-second Street and Broadway, one could
now see the great central pavilion through which passengers would move,
102 feet wide and nearly 76 feet high, fronted by a double row of ten
columns rising 35 feet. Above the columns stood an entablature adorned
with Adolph Weinman's stone maidens; a hollow circle would soon support
a clock with a dial seven feet in diameter.

New Yorkers were told that their new station had been built at a cost of $90 million, that twenty-eight acres of land had been cleared, eight of which would be occupied by the station building. They were told that there would be sixteen miles of track under the station and its approaches. They heard about the 45,000 tons of steel and the 620 concrete piers on which the marble columns would rest. Every figure and every dimension stretched the imagination of people who had just begun to live with electric trolleys and twenty-story skyscrapers.

A feeling of immense anticipation swept over the city as the great station took shape. Through the winter and into the spring, work on the exterior moved quickly. In late May one could walk past what had been an enormous pit and now see the station's shell. Most of the granite facade was in place, and all that was left to do of the exterior work was the huge steel-and-glass dome.

Meanwhile, work on the tunnels was coming to completion. In March 1909, as the station facade began to take form, the crosstown tunnels were finished. Wooden roadways were removed, and the residents of the town houses once more had New York City asphalt on their streets. The Hudson tubes, lined with concrete, were ready now for the tracks, signals, and the Westinghouse contractors to come in and electrify them.

The East River tunnels were slightly behind, as had been anticipated, with three of the four tubes nearly ready. The delay hardly mattered. On July 30 the president of the Long Island Railroad announced that commuters would be able to ride from Jamaica, Long Island, to Pennsylvania Station by Christmas!

On the day of this announcement the last piece of stone was positioned in Pennsylvania Station, officially completing exterior work. Half a mile of pink granite, transported by 1,140 freight cars from Milford, Massachusetts, shaped the great building. On either side of the massive main entrance were the carriageways, each the width of a city street, resembling in their stately proportions the arched driveways of the Louvre. It was said that while designing the station, Charles McKim kept pinned over his drawing table pictures of the facade of Sir John Soane's Bank of England and the Bernini colonnade enclosing the piazza of Saint Peter's. The Baths of Caracalla, particularly the tepidarium, remained ever with him when it came time to fashion the Great Room inside the station.

One could now walk close to the new station and peer into its eerie blackness. No carriages drove out of its carriageways yet; no full-skirted ladies or travel-bound gentlemen walked through colonnades. The structure that stood on eight of Manhattan's acres was still a magnificent promise.

CHAPTER ELEVEN

SOME SENTIMENTAL JOURNEYS

Charles McKim never saw the building he had designed. That spring he let it be known that he was leaving the city for his summer cottage on Long Island for a long rest. In fact, the architect was preparing for his death.

In June he gave up his town house on East Thirty-fifth Street, storing his furniture with his daughter. It had been hoped that this long rest would somehow begin to mend his damaged heart, but by midsummer his health had deteriorated rapidly, and on September 14, 1908, with his daughter at his bedside, Charles McKim died.

During these final months of finishing the inside of the new station and readying the tunnels for their new trains, inaugurations and ceremonies took place, not the grand ones that would come when the building was completely finished and the public would celebrate, but small, private occasions that became for those who were part of them sentimental journeys.

On the morning of November 18, 1909, James McCrea, president of the Pennsylvania Railroad, came to the Broad Street Station in Philadelphia with several railroad officials, including Samuel Rea, now second vice president of the railroad. The group boarded the presidential car in which Rea had often ridden with Cassatt.

At nine o'clock the train pulled out of Philadelphia, traveling its familiar route into New Jersey. One mile east of Newark, it suddenly veered from the path that customarily brought it to Exchange Place, on the edge of the Hudson. Today it traveled northeastward to a new station, appropriately named Manhattan Transfer. Here an electric locomotive would replace the steam engine for the ride through the tunnel and into Pennsylvania Station. The presidential train arrived at Manhattan Transfer at ten minutes to eleven, but since the tunnels under the Hudson had not yet been fully electrified, steam would have to be used on this run. To spare the dignitaries choking smoke fumes, the engine was placed behind the train instead of in front of it. It was the first and last time a steam locomotive took passengers through the Pennsylvania's tunnels.

The train continued along the new route, across six miles of Jersey Meadowlands, where most of the land excavated for the new station had been dumped, over a steel drawbridge that crossed the Hackensack River, through the rock of Bergen Hill, and then under the mile-wide Hudson.

By mid-July of 1909, when this picture was taken from the roof of Macy's, Pennsylvania Station was all but finished. The steel framework of the main waiting room is nearly complete. In the foreground, land has been cleared to build the Hotel Pennsylvania.

One of Adolph Weinman's four entablatures awaits its clock. The maiden holding the garland of sunflowers represents day; her sister, with the downcast eyes, night.

The train moved slowly through the tunnel, which was bone dry. The roadbed was smooth, and the illumination from a single string of electric lights bright enough to read a newspaper.

Twenty minutes after it had left Manhattan Transfer, the presidential train arrived in Pennsylvania Station. The men who ran the Pennsylvania Railroad, who had been involved in the execution of Alexander Cassatt's dream, now left their train and, for the first time, walked through the great building, their small steps echoing in the marble halls, their voices lost in all that silent space. It was not a place crowded with ghosts. It was new and unused, with nothing to fill its vast rooms but expectation.

At twenty minutes to one the directors boarded their train once again, proceeding through the tunnel beneath Manhattan and then under the East River. They arrived in Long Island City fourteen minutes later, having completed the journey Alexander Cassatt had begun eight years earlier.

Through the winter and into the spring, the remaining electrical work in the tunnels was pushed forward with all possible speed. In April 1910 electric trains were traveling from Pennsylvania Station to Jamaica as the

102

systems were being tested. The scheduled date for the first train to carry passengers under the rivers was August. And it was in August that the doors of the new station were to open to the world.

As the time drew near, intense anticipation swept the city. Parades and fireworks were planned for the day that the first passenger train would run under the East River, and towns all along Long Island, from Jamaica, in Queens, to the tiny villages near Montauk, were preparing their own celebrations. Brooklyn, never a place to be topped, was making sure its festivities would be louder, longer, and better than anyone else's. Representatives and specially selected citizens from various towns were invited to ride the first train out of Pennsylvania Station. Articles appeared regularly in all of New York's papers. On September 4 the *New York Times* devoted an entire section to the station's imminent opening. Every aspect of the work in progress was covered, along with its consequences, including the surge in real estate values along the main line of the Long Island Railroad.

While bands rehearsed and city officials polished their speeches, the Pennsylvania Railroad continued to test its equipment. By June the new station was finished, but because of a shortage of locomotives the opening had to be pushed back to September. Meanwhile, Samuel Rea had a copper box placed in a cornerstone of the new station. In it were architectural sketches together with annual reports and printed histories of the Pennsylvania Railroad's mammoth tunnel and terminal project.

In August 1910, a month before the public would finally see their new station, James McCrea once again boarded the presidential train in Philadelphia for the trip to New York. This time the party that accompanied him was considerably larger: seventy-eight gentlemen and two ladies. And their purpose was a somber one. It was a hot summer afternoon when the train pulled into Pennsylvania Station. The party, led by President McCrea and Samuel Rea, moved up from the platform onto the concourse and through the main waiting room. Lois Cassatt, accompanied by her two sons and daughter, was guided to the top of the grand stairway. There, in a niche, was the veiled statue of her husband.

DeWitt Cuyler, chairman of the memorial committee, spoke these words to President McCrea: "We ask you, as head of this great corporation, to take this statue into your keeping and to unveil it to the public eye so that all men may know, as the inscription so aptly tells, 'whose foresight, courage, and ability achieved the extension of the Pennsylvania Railroad System into New York City.' "

Cuyler pulled the veil from the statue. It was bronze, cast by Adolph A. Weinman, the sculptor Cassatt had commissioned to create the eagles that now perched above the Doric columns outside and who was part of the party assembled to pay homage to Cassatt. The statue caught with uncanny accuracy the attitude of the man, his intelligence, his strength, and the sensitivity that nurtured his vision.

There were more words about the man who had dreamed for so long of this station and the tunnels that would bring people into it. When the brief ceremony came to an end, the group descended the steps and crossed the main waiting room into the concourse. In the silence of the station Cuyler's last words hung in the air. "As the fitting conclusion to these ceremonies, I now declare this station officially opened."

A rare photograph of sculptor Adolph Weinman posing beside one of his keystones. The massive piece of ornamentation was duplicated several times on the interior and exterior of the station.

CHAPTER TWELVE

THE STATION HAS RISEN

That autumn of 1910 New Yorkers were brimming with excitement. Something wonderful was happening to their city, and they were about to witness it. They had come to expect that things done in New York would be grander and more magnificent than anywhere else, and there was no reason to believe that this time they would be disappointed.

Every New Year's Eve for the past six years, New Yorkers had stood beneath the soaring Times Tower, waiting for the stroke of midnight that would touch off a cascade of fireworks. Twenty-five years before, a bridge had been built for them across the East River so they could more easily commune with the people of Brooklyn. It was not just any bridge, but a visual and practical masterpiece so well known that for all who care to catalog achievements, Brooklyn Bridge became the eighth wonder of the world. Now, only a few days before the first Long Island train was scheduled to descend beneath the East River and pull into the new station, the *New York Times* proclaimed, in a September 4, 1910, editorial, the "Eve of an Era." Like Brooklyn Bridge, Pennsylvania Station was much more than an accommodation for travelers. It was a monumental gateway.

Although September 8 was the official opening of the new Pennsylvania Station, the only trains operating on that day were those of the Long Island Railroad, and only the part of the station that served the Long Island trains was open. It was not until two months later, on November 27, that full service began. On that Sunday throngs walked along Seventh Avenue from Times Square down to the entrance to the station. More than 100,000 sightseers and 25,000 westbound passengers would move through its doors before the day was over. The first long-distance train out of Pennsylvania Station was the *Chicago Special*, leaving at 8:04 A.M. After that, at 10:56, the famed *Pennsylvania Special* started on its run to Chicago. Eighty-nine trains left the station that day, forty-three headed east to Long Island and forty-six west to other parts of America.

Even the most blasé New Yorkers were impressed by the realization that they could now go over to Seventh Avenue and Thirty-third Street and board a train that would take them as far away as Louisiana without their having to get off until it pulled into New Orleans. But it was not only this new miracle of travel that brought the people here on that Sunday morning. They had come to see their station, the one they had watched being built

With its coffered, vaulted ceiling and its six-story-high Corinthian columns, the main waiting room was just what it was meant to be: the power of the Pennsylvania Railroad made manifest. It was also austere: in all that space—the room was about the size of the nave of St. Peter's in Rome—there was not a single bench on which to wait.

Right: In the gentlemen's waiting room male passengers could pass the time beneath the ornate ceiling and cast iron chandeliers in a space that suggested a small chapel. The door at the right leads to the smoking room; the other doors to the lavatory, barbershop, and bootblack.

Below: The broad sweep of the Grand Staircase leads from the main waiting room to the arcade beyond.

METRO-NORTH COMMUTER RAIL COMPANY

Left: Between their waiting room and their lavatory women passengers could alight in their retiring room.

Below: The arcade's elegant shops had metal fronts that were separated by columns of honey-colored travertine marble.

for the past six years. When the doors of the great building opened, there were 2,000 people waiting to come inside. What they saw did not disappoint them.

"The station," said the *Times* ". . . is the largest and handsomest in the world. Any idea of it formed from description and pictures falls short of the impression it makes upon the eye."

The exterior design was a Roman Doric colonnade, thirty-five feet high, surmounted by a low attic. The attic was broken by pavilions of varying size to indicate the principal entranceways. Above the four entrances the entablatures were now in place. Encircled by granite wreaths and flanked by sets of maidens were the huge clocks, seven feet in diameter. Adolph Weinman's eagles perched on either side of the maidens. At the north and south ends of the Seventh Avenue entrance, porticoed carriageways, thematically related to the Brandenburg Gate, in Berlin, gave passengers driving up to the station the sense of arrival in a major city.

Inside, the terminal was made up of several interconnected structures, each with its own architectural character. Through the Doric colonnade at the Seventh Avenue entrance, beyond the vestibule, passengers arriving on foot entered the arcade, a long, high-ceilinged boulevard lined on either side with shops. Above the shops, lunette windows close to the vaulted ceiling admitted light, the beams crisscrossing as they shone down on the marble floors. The shops in the arcade were fashioned of metal, with columns of travertine marble separating them. McKim had chosen the honey-colored stone not only for its warm, sunny tones but for its open texture, which gave character and distinction to the surface. Travertine also takes on a luster when rubbed, making it one of those rare materials that is enhanced by wear.

One hundred thousand people came to see the new station on opening day, November 27, 1910. Here some are gathered in the concourse to watch the first trains arrive and depart on the tracks below.

CULVER PICTURES

At the end of the arcade passengers entered the loggia, a colonnaded vestibule that served as an approach to the main waiting room. To one side of the loggia, facing south, was a formal dining room and café, large enough to accommodate five hundred people. Opposite the dining room, on the north side of the station, was a lunchroom and coffee shop. It was also in this area, at the top of the steps, that one came upon two niches carved into the travertine. One held the statue of Alexander Cassatt; the other would remain empty until 1930, when it received a statue of his indispensable lieutenant, Samuel Rea.

Standing at the head of the Grand Stairway, the people who came on this Sunday looked out across the vast space of the main waiting room, modeled on the tepidarium of the Baths of Caracalla. Built almost entirely of travertine, this room was an immense cathedral clerestory. Its plaster ceiling, painted to blend with the travertine, was studded with octagonal coffers ten feet across. Eight lunette windows close to the coffered ceilings bathed the room in ever-changing light. Beneath the windows Jules Guerin had painted enormous topographical maps of the Pennsylvania Railroad's territory in shades of blue and buff. Marble pedestals with iron candelabra stood in double rows along the floor, providing the main source of artificial light. Ticket and telegraph offices, also made from marble, appeared to be carved from a single piece of stone. There was serenity in this room, enhanced by the warm elegance of the travertine. As in the great cathedrals of Europe, the separate elements of Pennsylvania Station coalesced into a unified form that embraced the human spirit.

The opening-day sightseers continued on, descending the stairway and crossing the Great Room, passing two other stairways on the north and south ends of the room leading to the Thirty-first and Thirty-third Street entrances. Each stairway, approached by a bridge over the carriageway, was flanked by six Ionic columns.

At the west end of the main waiting room were two subsidiary waiting rooms, one for men and the other for women, each provided with long wooden benches. Off the ladies' waiting room was a lavatory, approached through a retiring room. The gentlemen's waiting room led to a lavatory, a changing room, and a barbershop.

If sightseers had been awed by the grandeur of the main waiting room, the concourse, with its enormous steel arches sweeping dramatically against the glass roof, gave one the unmistakable feeling that this was a place of journeys. It was a room of blacks and whites and shadows, a room meant to be filled with grit and memories. Here, the great clocks hung in the melancholy space, pointing the time with black iron hands. Here, the conductor's wail "All aboar-rrd!" could be as haunting as a train whistle in the night. One could look down below through the iron gates and see the trains coming in and pulling out. There was motion in this room, motion and anticipation. "The *Crescent Li-mi-ted* for New Or-le-ans boarding now!" A sense of faraway places hung in the air. In this train shed the mind journeyed long before the traveler set foot inside a train.

To achieve this highly subjective feeling of motion and drama, McKim designed the concourse with great precision, paying particular attention to the magnificent steel-and-glass roof. Although he modeled it after the great iron train sheds of Europe, his use of intersecting arched vaults produced

Opposite: A line of cars and taxis awaits passengers in one of the station's two carriageways. The bridge above carried pedestrians into the main waiting room.

Above: Even the lunchroom, where those pressed for time could grab a quick sandwich, had an air of grandeur and formality.

Left: McKim put as much care into the design of the train indicators as he did into every other element of the station.

Above: The drama and the complexity of McKim's steel-and-glass concourse roof remain undiminished in this photograph, taken during Pennsylvania Station's final days.

Right: Unlike the waiting room, where all was classical restraint and severity, the concourse, with its bare structural steel, suggested the motion and power of the modern age. McKim patterned his roof on the iron train sheds of Europe but demanded more intricacy in its design. If the station's other rooms were Roman, this one was pure American.

The U.S. government liked what it saw of McKim's plans well enough to award his architectural firm the commission for its new General Post Office in Manhattan. Completed in 1913, the building's Corinthian columns faced Pennsylvania Station's Doric ones from across Eighth Avenue.

a more structurally complicated design than its European counterparts. Here is where McKim's great sense of detail shone. Because he wanted to avoid visual monotony, an intricate pattern of latticed steel had to be developed to incorporate the varied sizes of the arches. The project was further complicated by McKim's insistence that there be no exposed ties along the arches. This proviso called for a costly cantilever arch anchored to the surrounding structure. The room itself was a granite-walled courtyard surmounted by the three intersecting steel barrel arches of the magnificent roof.

With acute attention to detail, the train indicators, placed at the boarding gates, had been specially designed to conform to the ornate iron fencing that enclosed the platform area. Each indicator stood sixteen feet high and was of cast-iron painted black. The aluminum sign cards, which displayed the name of the train as well as its stops, were painted bright red, the only touch of color in this room of black and gray.

Along the Eighth Avenue wall of the concourse were four stories of offices used by the executive staff of the Pennsylvania Railroad. Here, too, were medical rooms, a special room for funeral parties, and the station's police department.

The station rested on two city blocks; yet one was never confused by its vastness. One progressed easily from the European elegance of the arcade to the opulent grandeur of the main waiting room and then to the drama and movement of the concourse. McKim's brilliance was evident in his ability to break up the spaces so that each was a different experience and yet all were related.

The station conceived as a visual masterpiece was also planned to function with greatest efficiency. It was the first terminal designed to provide for the separation of incoming and outgoing traffic. An exit concourse built between the main concourse and the train platforms ensured uninterrupted movement of arriving as well as departing passengers. When a passenger arrived at Pennsylvania Station, he made his exit from this concourse directly to the side streets. The two carriageways, which ran parallel to the main waiting room along either side of the Seventh Avenue entrance, were also divided: incoming vehicles entered through the south side; departing ones exited from the north carriageway. Both carriageways admitted access to the main waiting room, where ticket offices stood diagonally across from one another, and to the main baggage room, located on the same level as the main waiting room, beneath the arcade. Baggage was delivered to and from trains through a special subway.

Because the station had to provide for commuters coming from Long Island as well as travelers from farther away, part of the terminal was set aside exclusively for the Long Island Railroad. At the northern end, below Thirty-third Street, a separate waiting room with ticket offices and other facilities served commuters without unnecessary encounters with long-distance travelers.

When the Pennsylvania Railroad commissioned its station, the United States government took the opportunity to build a much-needed post office across the street on Eighth Avenue. The Pennsylvania's trains carried about 40 percent of the mail originating in New York City, and the government bought a four-hundred-square-foot plot from the railroad and built its new post office directly over the Pennsy tracks. The firm of McKim, Mead and White was delighted to be awarded the commission for the new post office building: it is rare for an architectural firm to get the opportunity to design a building that will complement in appearance and function one they have just completed.

As with Pennsylvania Station the new post office would consist of a row of columns, this time Corinthian, running north to south. At either end of the building would be pavilions containing niches. The architectural style of the post office, according to McKim, Mead and White's description, would be Roman Corinthian, while that of Pennsylvania Station was Roman Doric. Below the post office and Pennsylvania Station an elaborate conveyor system with drop chutes would move the mail between the two buildings with no need for trucks.

Though buildings such as these brought New York into the new century, when the post office was completed one could walk the Eighth Avenue block from Thirty-third to Thirty-second streets and imagine that this was not twentieth-century Manhattan at all but ancient Rome and that one was not dodging harried New Yorkers but strolling along the via Appia.

Less than a decade earlier, ferries spilled travel-weary passengers onto the congested shores of Manhattan. Now they entered the magic city through a temple of glass, steel, and marble. Everything grand and beautiful and uplifting about this place was designed for the man or woman who caught a train. One could not walk through the building without a restless urge tugging at one's spirit. In exciting such feeling Cassatt and McKim achieved their great success. This place of journeys remained in our souls long after our journeys were complete.

CHAPTER THIRTEEN

THE NEW STATION ENTERS THE TWENTIETH CENTURY

When Pennsylvania Station was conceived the country had barely left the nineteenth century. By 1910, the year it opened, the country was beginning its thrust into the twentieth century. But most people still clung to the habits and accoutrements of the 1800s.

Charles McKim had this era in mind when he designed two separate waiting rooms. The ladies', with its connecting retiring room, had a matron on duty to attend to the needs of female passengers. Across the way the gentlemen's waiting room accommodated smokers; it went without question that women never indulged. In a description published when the station was opened, much was made of the gentlemen's changing room, where "Mr. Commuter" could engage a small chamber with toilet facilities enclosed by glass partitions and supplied with soap, towels, and a silver-handled whisk. Here he could check his suitcase and change into his tails for a dinner or a theater engagement, thus avoiding the inconvenience of a trip to his club.

The sexually segregated auxiliary waiting rooms were not the only genuflection to nineteenth-century tastes. If the main waiting room was awesome and exquisitely designed, it could also be intimidating, with its marble pedestals whose bases alone were taller than the average person. In this room of wondrous space there were no seats at all, and early pictures show Lilliputians clustered around the marble pedestals, sometimes sitting on their luggage for want of a bench.

But if, in this Belle Epoque palace where style sometimes overshadowed ease, one had to separate from one's spouse in order to sit down, there were other accommodations that bespoke the comforts of a genteel society. The Corinthian Room, a formal dining area, served tea from silver pots. On the first floor, in the offices of the concourse, there was an engagement room where people coming in from out of town could hold private meetings. Nearby, a special room for funeral parties was available. The Travelers Aid Society maintained an office in the station to assist confused or stranded passengers.

And of course there were the trains. Into and out of this magnificent building the Pennsylvania ran its fleet of supertrains, one more prestigious than the next. The *Florida Special* and the *Miamian* took wealthy vacationers South. The *Congressional Limited*, pride of the New York–Washington

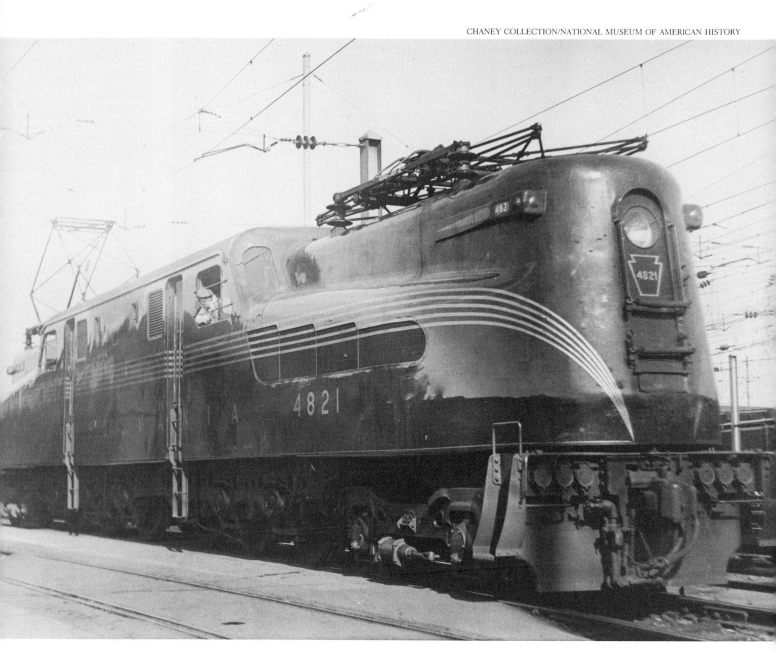

Perhaps the best-known electric locomotives ever built, the GG-1s symbolized the Pennsylvania Railroad's early and vigorous commitment to electrification. Raymond Loewy designed the engines, calling for sleek, rivet-free construction and painting them a magnificent Brunswick green with gold striping. The first GG-1s went into service in 1935; geared for ninety miles per hour, they proved strong and reliable. Eventually the line ordered one hundred and thirty of them, and some stayed in service through the 1970s.

Above: With its tall windows and Italian-walnut furniture, the formal dining room was as impressive as the rest of the station. Originally called the Corinthian Room, it became the Savarin Restaurant in 1929.

Right: Maiden voyage—the first Pennsylvania Railroad train leaves the new station on November 27, 1910.

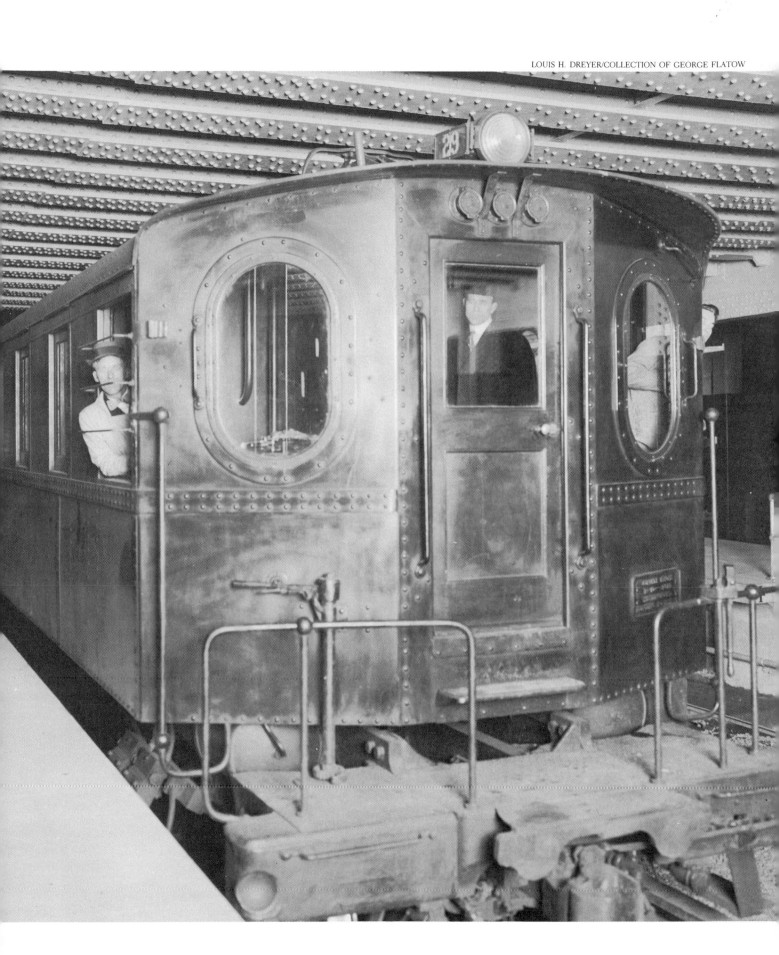

run, left daily. There was the *Crescent Limited*, to New Orleans, and the *Havana Special*, so called because it traveled as far south as the Florida Keys, from which passengers could hop a boat to Cuba. Later on, in the forties, the *Havana Special* was converted to a mail train, making stops in the Carolinas and Georgia before reaching Florida. It also became the train of poor blacks traveling to and from the South, some of whom stood all the way. They often brought along fried chicken lunches, and the debris left behind after each trip prompted the nickname *The Chicken Bone*.

Then there was the train that made the New York–Chicago run. The flagship of the luxury fleet, it set out on its maiden voyage as the *Pennsylvania Special* under the watchful eye of Alexander Cassatt before Pennsylvania Station existed. Now the *Broadway Limited*, its name was synonymous with glamour and celebrity. Each day the *Broadway* could be found on its track an hour before it was scheduled to leave, its carpeting vacuumed, silver polished, and fresh flowers placed in the dining car. A 1939 *Fortune* magazine article illustrated the pride that the Pennsylvania Railroad took in the *Broadway* as it was readied for service in Sunnyside Yard:

> There Polish and Negro women in bloomers swarm into it with mops and brooms, and men from the commissary supply its diner with six waiters, four cooks, a pantryman, a dishwasher, a steward, and food. The train may stay in Sunnyside Yard for two to eight hours, perhaps on adjoining tracks with Paul Block's *Friendship*, Barbara Hutton Haugwit-Reventlow's *Curley Hut*, or the *Ranger*, the private car on which Eleanor Patterson maintains a permanent crew.

The *Broadway Limited* was an all-Pullman train with no inexpensive coaches, consisting of sleeping and parlor cars staffed by a barber and a stenographer in addition to a piano player in the observation lounge. It was the train of presidents and kings and of movie stars who usually connected in Chicago with the Santa Fe's *Chief, El Capitan*, or *California Limited*, all of which were destined for Los Angeles. The notables who boarded the *Broadway* included Charlie Chaplin and Will Rogers, Ethel Barrymore and Albert Einstein, Duke Ellington and Count Basie, the Duke and the Duchess of Windsor and President Franklin D. Roosevelt, Sergei Rachmaninoff and Leopold Stokowski.

The eccentricities of its famous passengers became well known to the staff. Enrico Caruso, for example, did not like to board until the train was just about to leave. While other passengers were getting on he would pace back and forth in the concourse, occasionally taking a pinch from one of his elegant snuff boxes. Sophie Tucker was so enamored of the food on the *Broadway Limited* that she never boarded without greeting the kitchen staff and sampling their specialties. In the twenties, the *Broadway's* galley was staffed by four cooks, who prepared as many as twenty-four different dishes.

The supertrains required a sort of goodwill ambassador to usher such stellar passengers through the station and see to their needs. That someone was Bill Egan, the first stationmaster to work in the new terminal and one of the most famous personalities ever to work for the railroad. Egan was a tall, attractive Irishman who dressed for his job in top hat, gloves, and tails.

He was nicknamed Big Bill because he was, according to those who worked with him, as big as the station. His office in the concourse, directly above track 17, was a sanctuary where presidents and movie stars could sit and listen to his stories while waiting for their trains. Teddy Roosevelt used Bill Egan's typewriter to compose editorials for *Outlook* magazine. FDR was a friend of Egan's, and in his days as New York governor he would drop into Bill's office to chat whenever he had to catch a train to his home at Hyde Park.

A story repeated in the *New York Times* on September 1, 1943, at the time of Egan's death, gives some idea of his ability to put all people at their ease: "When the Duke of Windsor, the Prince of Wales, visited the country, Bill sauntered across the station, his topper set at rakish angle and his mahogany cane dangling from his left arm. Extending his huge hand he said, 'How are you, Prince? What can I do for you?'" The story goes that Bill Egan and the Duke of Windsor were fast friends thereafter.

Through the years the wall behind Egan's huge oak desk was filled with hundreds of letters and signed photographs from the celebrities who knew him. Egan was less a public relations man than a person who simply understood human nature. The *Times* said he summed up his feelings about people in the words of Polonius: "Give every man thine ear, but few thy voice; / Take each man's censure, but reserve thy judgement." Eight hundred people attended Bill Egan's funeral, including an honor guard of redcaps. Eleanor and Franklin Roosevelt sent flowers.

Like many of the station's early employees, Egan loved his job and the railroad that employed him. In those days of good profits, people who worked in Pennsylvania Station were treated with extraordinary consideration. In the concourse, on the fourth floor of the offices located along the Eighth Avenue entrance, the railroad had installed a gym and a lounge under the auspices of the Pennsylvania Railroad Young Men's Christian Association, complete with a library, a billiard room, and a bowling alley. There were also showers and baths and enough beds to accommodate one hundred and seventy-five trainmen and other railroad employees who needed to stay overnight in New York. Wherever station employees had to stand to do their jobs—in the kitchens, elevators, cigar stands, ticket offices—cork flooring eased the load on their legs. In all, eleven thousand square feet of cork was installed by the railroad for the comfort of its employees.

During the first few years of its existence, Pennsylvania Station served a civilized nation with grace and dignity. But there were omens that the glory days of the Pennsylvania Railroad were behind it. In 1913 Samuel Rea became ninth president of the company, succeeding James McCrea, who had presided since Cassatt's death. By now the days of expansion were over. Notwithstanding the gym and the cork flooring Pennsylvania Station employees were beginning to demand better wages and working conditions. By 1915, with Europe at war, the cost of materials the railroad needed rose sharply due in part to the enormous overseas demand for American goods.

On March 9, 1917, Samuel Rea dedicated Gustav Lindenthal's New York Connecting Bridge, the last segment of the Pennsylvania Railroad's extension into New York. A month later, on April 6, the United States entered World War I. The war effort depended heavily on the railroads

Right: Bill Egan, *probably the world's most famous stationmaster, sits in his Pennsylvania Station office in the 1920s. Behind him on the wall are photographs of a few of the movie stars and heads of state he shepherded through his station.*

Below: Charlie Chaplin takes *breakfast aboard the* Broadway Limited, *the Pennsylvania's elegant rival to the New York Central's* Twentieth Century Limited.

that would carry troops and supplies to the East Coast and the ships that would take them to Europe. On December 26, 1917, President Woodrow Wilson issued a proclamation placing all railroads, including the Pennsylvania, under federal control. William McAdoo, the man who had built the H&M tunnels and who was now Wilson's son-in-law, was made director-general in charge of the railroads. For almost three years, the government ran the nation's trains.

Many men who worked for the Pennsylvania Railroad went into the Army, and for the first time women were mobilized to fill their places. In Pennsylvania Station some were given jobs as dispatchers and ticket sellers, although for the most part women were kept out of sight, taking reservations by phone and performing other tasks behind the scenes.

Frills were eliminated; the supertrains, including the legendary *Broadway Limited*, were stripped of their glamorous trappings and used to transport troops. The war had come not only to the Pennsylvania Railroad but to its station as well. A federal order authorized the Red Cross to feed troops in transit and provide emergency relief. Canteens equipped with rolling kitchens and medical supplies were set up in the country's railroad stations. One soldier, remembering what it was like to pass through Pennsylvania Station, wrote a poem and sent it to the Red Cross:

Ethel Barrymore poses with the engineer of the Broadway Limited *before setting out for Chicago sometime during the 1930s.*

> As we left New York agoing forth,
> Today to fight for the Land of Worth,
> We made a pause in "Pennsy" while
> The Red Cross girl with cheery smile
> Brought to us a postcard there
> To lighten home folks' worried care—
> An apple too and a cigarette—
> But the farewell smile we'll not forget,
> For the 'couraging smile of the women here
> Will win the war—now get that clear,
> For the soldier knows that he must fight
> To keep that smile forever bright.

When the government returned the railroads to their owners at war's end, the Pennsylvania was in sorry shape. The neglected roads were in terrible condition, and the trains needed major overhauling. Money for the work was not forthcoming from a country whose economy had slid into a postwar recession. True, the flagship of the railroad, the *Broadway Limited*, was back on its usual New York–Chicago run and sparkling once again. But passengers who were not riding one of the showcase trains could see the results of financial strain all too clearly. The trains showed signs of wear and tear, and throughout the operations there was a general feeling of things not having been kept up.

It was not until 1920 that the effects of the war seemed finally to recede into the country's past. In that year, more people traveled on Pennsylvania trains than in any previous year, and much of the passenger traffic was coming into Pennsylvania Station. By year's end nearly thirty-eight million people had passed through the station, three times the number that had used it when it first opened.

If the economic conditions brought on by World War I had vanished, there were subtler changes that would leave more permanent marks on the American psyche. Prohibition, become law on January 16, 1920, forced drinking Americans to imbibe clandestinely, and New York City became a mecca of nightclubs and speakeasies owned by organized crime. The pace of the city was faster than ever. Theatergoers filled the seats of Broadway houses, and almost every nightclub in town had people waiting at the door for a table. In Bill Egan's office a photo of Texas Guinan, Queen of the Nightclubs, shared space with presidents and heads of state.

Each Friday evening the *Cannon Ball* left Pennsylvania Station and headed toward Montauk along Long Island's Gold Coast, just as it had done since the station's first days. But the all-Pullman train that had formerly carried wealthy dowagers to their summer cottages now rocked with Jazz Age partygoers who frolicked in the country, returning each Sunday evening on the *Cannon Ball* into the quiet spaces of Pennsylvania Station.

During the twenties the number of passengers using the station increased by 73 percent. Although the volume of traffic suggests that the railroad was in fine shape the statistics are deceptive. The general prosperity of the decade masked the fact that the railroad was on the edge of a great decline.

When Pennsylvania Station was built, railroading had reached its zenith, and no one foresaw the end of the line. The automobile was still a toy of the rich, and its impact on transportation had not yet begun. By the twenties, however, it was apparent that cars, trucks, and buses would reach for some of the passengers and freight that had hitherto belonged exclusively to the railroads.

An event that ignited the American spirit at a time when the country needed a hero also was prelude to the eventual eclipse of the great railroads. In May 1927 Charles Lindbergh flew his tiny *Spirit of St. Louis* across the Atlantic from New York to Paris. One year later, Amelia Earhart became the first woman to cross the Atlantic in a plane. The country thereafter was so caught up in the romance of the airplane that in 1929 the Pennsylvania joined with the Santa Fe railroad and Transcontinental Air Transport, Inc., to inaugurate an air-rail service between New York City and Los Angeles. The ambitious cross-country trip seemed to be higher on adventure than comfort—westbound passengers would take a train to Columbus, Ohio, then a plane to Waynoka, Oklahoma, another train to Clovis, New Mexico, and finally, a plane to Los Angeles; but the Pennsylvania spared nothing in publicizing its new service. The official inauguration day was heralded with enough pomp and ceremony to install a president. In Los Angeles Mary Pickford christened the first eastbound flight. Called the *City of Los Angeles* the plane was piloted as far as Winslow, Arizona, by Lindbergh himself. The following day, Lindbergh flew another plane from Winslow back to Los Angeles, where Gloria Swanson christened it the *City of Philadelphia*.

In New York, Pennsylvania Station was the starting point of the East Coast celebrations. A Ford trimotor similar to those that would make the coastal trips was displayed in the main waiting room. At an elaborate ceremony broadcast by local radio stations, Amelia Earhart broke a bottle of champagne across the propeller, christening the plane the *City of New*

York. With nineteen other passengers Earhart led the way to the concourse, from which a train took them on the first leg of their trip.

But even the romance of the airplane could not overcome the impracticalities of taking trains to planes to trains and planes again. Passengers were at the mercy of the weather, and missed connections sometimes added hours to already long and arduous journeys. After a few years the railroad gave up the idea, selling its shares in Transcontinental Air Transport, which would reemerge a few years later as TWA.

The air-rail plan was a victim not only of its impracticality but of an economic storm that would ground the embryonic air industry for nearly a decade. In October 1929 the Great Depression whirled in like a tornado. In its wake princes of finance became paupers, and institutions that seemed as sound as the earth itself were blown away. In 1929, a year when close to sixty-six million passengers used Pennsylvania Station, the railroad's stock was worth $110 a share; by 1932 the price had fallen to $6.50. E. Y. Harburg's lyrics to Jay Gorney's tune of that year told it all:

> *Once I built a railroad, made it run,*
> *Made it race against time.*
> *Once I built a railroad. Now it's done.*
> *Brother, can you spare a dime?*

By 1933 the country was deep into the Depression. As in other cities clusters of shanties, nicknamed Hoovervilles, sprang up along the edges of Manhattan's rivers. Prohibition had been repealed, but few people could afford the good times and high living that was Broadway in the twenties. Legitimate theaters converted to movie houses, providing affordable entertainment to those fortunate enough to have jobs. Now the great station, once the gilded hall of Charles McKim's elegant ladies, became a hostel for the homeless. William Faulkner, in a short story called "Pennsylvania Station," wrote:

> In the rotunda, where the people appeared as small and intent as ants, the smell and sense of snow still lingered, though high now among the steel girders, spent and vitiated too and filled here with a weary and ceaseless murmuring, like the voices of pilgrims upon the infinite plain, like the voices of all the travelers who have ever passed through it . . .

How secure and permanent those travertine walls must have seemed to those who could hardly believe in tomorrow. To be in a place where people still had places to go and the means to get there must have been a promise, however bittersweet, of better days ahead.

For those who could still afford to take trains, it was a time of futuristic luxury. If the age of the airplane was hovering in the skies, it seemed that some of those silver birds had actually landed on the Pennsylvania's tracks. On November 1, 1928, the railroad announced an enormous electrification program that would eventually convert all of its tracks east of Harrisburg, Pennsylvania, to electric traction; steam engines could be replaced by more economical electric locomotives. The costly and complicated program was to be accomplished in a span of seven or eight years.

No one could have foretold on that autumn day that one year later the Pennsylvania Railroad would be fighting for its economic life. Nevertheless what may have seemed impossible during the terrible years that followed 1929 was finally accomplished. By 1934 the Pennsy had produced the GG-1, its electric locomotive prototype. The railroad had chosen the French-born industrial designer Raymond Loewy to create its new engine. Loewy, whose first assignment for the Pennsylvania Railroad had been to redesign the trash cans in Pennsylvania Station, rejected the standard technique of riveting together the train's body and instead had the entire shell welded. The result was a sleek design whose startlingly simple horizontal lines suggested drama and great speed. The railroad was so impressed by Loewy's work that they commissioned him to put his futuristic imprint on everything from signal towers to train interiors.

During the 1930s the Broadway Limited *was reequipped with a fleet of modern, lightweight stainless-steel cars, whose amenities models are enjoying in these publicity photographs. As the scene out the window suggests, this observation car is standing motionless in the Pennsylvania's yards.*

METRO-NORTH COMMUTER RAIL COMPANY

Loewy, who redesigned such star trains as the *Admiral*, the *Spirit of St. Louis*, and the *Broadway Limited*, had artistic control over everything from sleeping compartments to coffee cups and toothpick wrappers.

Other designers were also introducing sleek new streamlined trains made of lightweight stainless steel with wide windows, diffused lighting, and elaborate lounge cars. For the first time, fold-up beds were installed in compartments to give passengers private roomettes. Air-conditioning had been introduced, first in dining cars and eventually throughout many long-distance trains. The *Broadway Limited* was among those to be completely reequipped. To see such glistening silver creatures speeding into the night made it difficult to believe that the country was gripped by financial disaster.

In the Sunnyside yards a cleaning staff continued to wash, sweep, and vacuum each train that came into Pennsylvania Station. A huge warehouse stored the meats, groceries, linens, and silverware for the dining cars. Inside, butchers cut up meat, inspectors checked the produce that was to be prepared

The models seem slightly less frozen in this view of the lounge car, and the lowered blinds prevent another stationary trackside scene from dampening the effect.

METRO-NORTH COMMUTER RAIL COMPANY

The Pennsylvania hauled a Ford trimotor into the station to promote its air-rail route between New York and Los Angeles when the service began, in 1929.

on the trains, and chefs were specially trained in the "dummy diner," a mock-up of a real dining car kitchen. Seamstresses mended napkins and tablecloths before sending them to the laundry. There was even a "tomato ripener," whose job it was to shoot up tomatoes with ethylene gas so they would be ready for the salad chef.

By 1936 the economy was beginning to climb out of the worst of the Depression, and a feeling of optimism began to ease back into the American

spirit. In the late thirties an organ was installed in the station's main waiting room to play carols at Christmas time. Briefly the station hired a bugler for the sole purpose of announcing the evening departure of the *Broadway Limited*, whose New York–Chicago running time had been reduced to seventeen hours. Each evening he stood at the foot of the Grand Stairway and began his march through the main waiting room and the concourse, blowing his bugle as he approached track 13. Redcaps, seeing him approach, leaped to attention and shouted: "*Broadway Limited*, leaving at six P.M. from track number thirteen!"

Pennsylvania Station was a bustling hub of activity. Nearly 3,000 people worked there, 2,200 of whom were railroad employees; 335 redcaps stood ready to assist travelers with their luggage. In the reservations room the famous Pennsylvania 6-2000 telephone number rang out on the average of 700 times an hour, requiring 20 clerks to answer questions. Another 76 clerks sold tickets. The lost-and-found department, with its miscellany of cats, crutches, and lost umbrellas, attested to the fact that human beings were still going about the business of being imperfectly human.

In 1936 about 176,000,000 people passed in and out of Pennsylvania Station, many of them on the Long Island Railroad. The shabby summer-traffic road that Alexander Cassatt bought when he decided to build his station now carried more passengers than any other line in the country, including the Pennsylvania itself.

Pennsylvania Station was changing with the times. The restaurant and coffee shops were now run by the Savarin Corporation, the restaurateurs who had been in the Waldorf-Astoria on Thirty-third Street before it was demolished in 1929 to make way for the Empire State Building. Lucius Boomer, the famed chef of the Waldorf, was in charge of all the kitchens in Pennsylvania Station. In addition to the coffee shops and restaurant, Savarin had a cocktail lounge in the arcade, where the clock was set five minutes fast for the benefit of commuters who lingered too long over their drinks. Other changes, like the beverage-dispensing machines that dotted the marble floors in the arcade, reflected a faster-paced society. The men who once strolled through the arcade with bowler hats and walking sticks now drank thirty-five-cent martinis in the station's Clover Leaf Bar before catching the train home. As a further accommodation to Mr. Commuter, an escalator now ran up the center of the Grand Stairway.

By 1937 the former governor who used to drop by Bill Egan's office on his way to Hyde Park was serving his second term as President of the United States, and a country just emerging from the trauma of the Great Depression was growing increasingly uneasy over events in Europe. Just a year earlier Hitler's army had goose-stepped its way across the Rhineland. Now Japan was growing militant, while Mussolini and Franco were allying themselves with Hitler.

Pennsylvania Station had lived through the remnants of a gilded age, a world war, and a depression. But it would be the people who would pass through the station within the next few years that would make it forevermore the place of intense, bittersweet memory. It would begin on a Sunday morning in December.

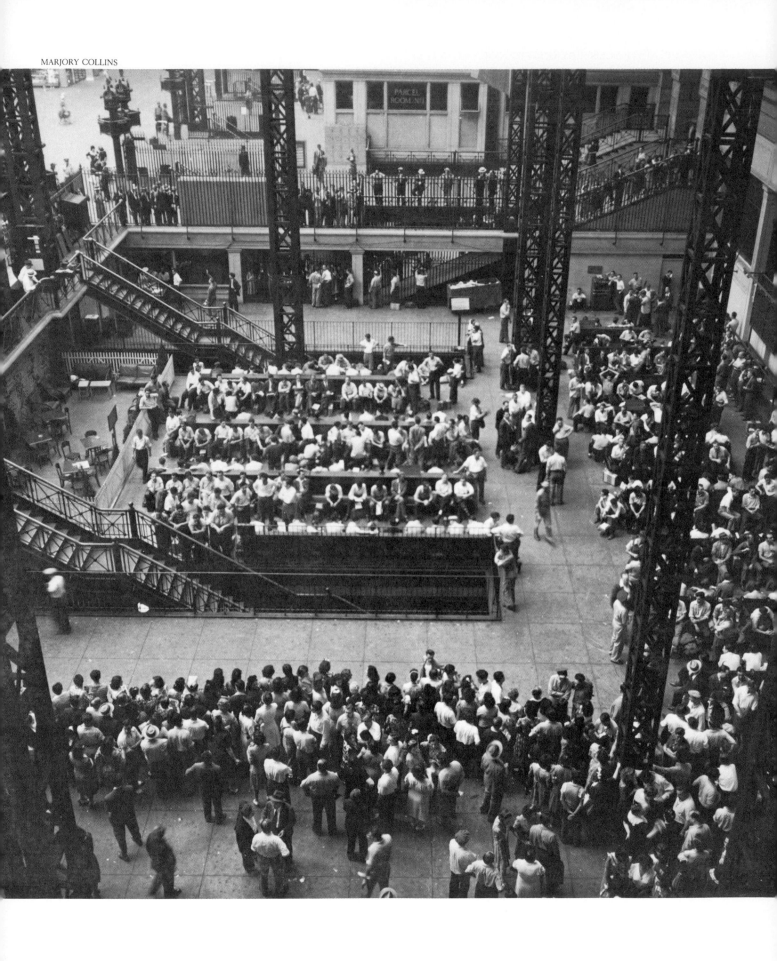

MARJORY COLLINS

CHAPTER FOURTEEN

PENNSYLVANIA STATION GOES TO WAR

A cold, overcast Sunday afternoon in Manhattan. In Pennsylvania Station the usual number of passengers milled about the concourse, some waiting to board the *Silver Meteor*, leaving at 2:05 for Florida. Others had just arrived from Washington on the 1:50. The piles of newspapers at the eight Union newsstands had dwindled considerably. It was December 7, 1941, and the headline on the *New York Times* read:

ROOSEVELT APPEALS TO HIROHITO
AFTER NEW THREAT IN INDOCHINA

Upstairs in the arcade, strollers were window shopping at Ryan's clothes shop or the Doubleday Bookstore. Some who had celebrated too much the night before were sitting at the counter of the Penn Drug Store, nursing Bromos and Alka Seltzers. At the nearby Clover Leaf Bar, customers drank beer and listened to the WOR broadcast of the New York Giants football game at the Polo Grounds. At 2:25 the first bulletin broke in:

FLASH! WASHINGTON—THE WHITE HOUSE
ANNOUNCES JAPANESE ATTACK ON PEARL HARBOR

The next day, as shock and disbelief turned to anger and thoughts of revenge, recruiting offices throughout the country were jammed with men eager to join up as the United States declared war on Japan. On December 11 Germany and Italy declared war on the United States.

New York City immediately began preparing for the war. The fire department was put on full alert in the event of air raid. Floodgates were installed at tunnel entrances against the threat of air attack or sabotage. All furloughs and leaves of servicemen were canceled.

More than ever before Pennsylvania Station became a palace of human movement. Men already in uniform crowded the concourse, catching the trains that would take them back to their bases. Others, newly recruited and still in civilian clothes, arrived at the station to be sent to one of the training camps in the country. Months later, having completed their training, the men would be back in the station, in uniform, ready for the next leg of their journey. Those destined to fight in the Pacific would connect with trains to the West Coast, while those going to Europe would board one of

Still in their civilian clothes, draftees wait in the concourse for the train that will take them to their induction center in August 1942.

131

the troopships—the reconverted *Queen Elizabeth* or *Queen Mary*—or one of the Liberty ships that crowded the Hudson.

Leonard Leader, a veteran who is currently visiting professor at UCLA's School of Journalism, spoke of Pennsylvania Station as it was on the day he left for a training camp:

> On October 28, 1942, I was one of hundreds boarding a Long Island Railroad train to go off to the army, to war in Europe, a journey which lasted nearly forty months. The scene that afternoon in Pennsylvania Station was one of a great mass of young men, all of us in civilian clothes, lined up in rough formation. My wife and mother succeeded in holding back tears. I had none, for I was proud to be going to fight Hitler. There was nothing more important in the world.
>
> But most etched in my mind is a stout woman with a wide face soaked in tears and distorted in anguish. The uncontrolled grief in her face seemed to dominate the station. Looking back, I think she must have understood more than we did.

Such scenes were repeated daily as young men gathered with their sweethearts and families in the concourse to say their goodbyes. Alfred Eisenstaedt, who shot a series of photographs in the concourse for *Life* magazine during the war years, recently looked over the pictures and recalled how painful the assignments were:

> I remember it was daylight. The light was beautiful—so subdued. The atmosphere in the station was sad and exciting, and many people were crying. The men were very shy—it was difficult for some of them to embrace in public. Their mothers couldn't go beyond the train gates, and they stood there, looking down at the tracks, crying. It was very difficult to focus and be unobtrusive. I was very tense and very emotional. This was over forty years ago, but I remember exactly the mood.

Day and night, soldiers and sailors came to the station. Sometimes they appeared in great masses, an entire unit deployed on the steps of the waiting room or in the concourse. Other times, especially in the early hours of the morning, a couple of soldiers and a sailor on leave would share a bench with a woman and her child. The station that had sheltered the homeless during the Great Depression was once again a hostel of sorts. Robert L. Riddell, now executive director of the USO, was working at the information desk in Penn Station when he returned from the war. Riddell had arrived home on a Friday after seeing action in Africa, Italy, and on Omaha Beach and was at work in the station the following Monday. Across the information desk, he looked into the faces of men who were going to the places from which he had just returned, seeing their apprehension and knowing, better than they could, what they would be facing. "It was a temple of emotions," he said. "Every emotion a human being could feel was experienced in that station, including loneliness. Here, you could be with ten thousand people and you could be totally dejected and alone."

If fear and pain and apprehension were the baggage carried by the men who were going off to war, the station could also be a place of respite and relief. The Savarin coffee shop, with its large seating capacity, soon became accustomed to feeding great numbers of troops. The USO distributed food coupons to soldiers who had to lay over at the station and downstairs, on the lower level, dispensed coffee and snacks in a servicemen's lounge. Occasionally, a celebrity coming through the station would stop at the canteen to chat with the men. The USO also maintained an information center in the main waiting room, and upstairs, in the women's retiring room, a pink-walled nursery had been installed with four cribs, two high chairs, an electric stove for warming bottles, and a refrigerator. A trained nurse and a matron were always in attendance to take care of the babies and small children of servicemen who wanted to spend some last moments alone with their wives.

Once again, employees of the Pennsylvania Railroad went off to war. In 1942 a banner was suspended in the main waiting room with two stars, a blue one representing the employees serving in the war, a gold one for those who had been killed. By the time the war ended twenty-five thousand railroad employees had served their country.

In 1945 Raymond Loewy, the man who had done so much to change the look of the Pennsylvania Railroad in the thirties, installed six huge photomurals, each forty feet high, on the west wall of the main waiting room, depicting a conductor, an engineer, a porter, a soldier, a sailor, and a marine, all symbolizing the railroad's service to the nation. Loewy also designed a sixty-foot American flag weighing two hundred pounds and made of fluorescent material, which hung in the area between the main waiting room and the concourse.

With so many railroad men called to war, the Pennsylvania again hired women to take their place. But this time these women were not kept out of sight. There were trainwomen on the trains in Pennsylvania Station and women ticket agents working in full view of passengers. Some were hired as ushers. Wearing navy serge skirts, white broadcloth shirts, and navy peaked caps, they opened gates, checked tickets, and directed passengers to their trains. And women began announcing trains. Ann Gavin's melodic Irish accent became an endearing fixture in the station, and she remained on the job long after the soldiers had come home.

Throughout the war, trains passed through the station with crack efficiency. This was due in large part to President Roosevelt's determination to avoid the mistakes of the Wilson administration during World War I, when the government takeover of the railroads nearly destroyed them. In 1938, with the possibility of United States involvement in a European conflict still remote in most American minds, FDR asked the presidents of the larger railroads to prepare a confidential report on how the railroads should be handled in the event of war. The president studied the recommendations of men like Frederic Williamson, who headed the New York Central, and Martin Clement, the Pennsylvania's president, realizing that they would know better than any federal bureaucrat how their companies would be able to function under war conditions.

On December 23, 1941, twenty-two days after the Japanese attack on Pearl Harbor, the Office of Defense Transportation was formed, with Joseph B. Eastman, a man familiar with railroading, as its head. Among the department's duties was coordination of federal agencies with private transportation groups to assure the orderly movement of troops and supplies.

Because of the Pennsylvania's electrification program, the railroad was

Above: In a scene from M-G-M's wartime romance The Clock, *Robert Walker and Judy Garland embrace at the top of the Grand Stairway, overlooking the main waiting room of the station.*

Left: Raymond Loewy began his association with Pennsylvania Station by designing its garbage cans. Later he went on to do the line's locomotives, and during the war he created the photo murals that flank the American flag in this 1945 view of the main waiting room.

Throughout the war soldiers and sailors, their leaves over, would catch a few minutes of uncomfortable sleep on the station's steps—as these men are in April 1944—while waiting for the train back to base.

well-equipped to handle the traffic demands of the war. Despite a scarcity of raw materials, the company was able to add 125 freight locomotives to its prewar inventory of 66. Thousands of old freight cars were rebuilt at an enormous cost that would have been unjustifiable in peacetime. The expansion and renovation did not extend, however, to passenger coaches, and as a result trains were always packed. With military needs taking priority, civilian passengers on regular trains often had to stand in the aisles.

As in World War I even the Pennsylvania's luxury trains were pressed into service. Some were converted into moving hospital wards, and for civilians who had a difficult enough time getting on any train a ride on one of the few functioning supertrains required knowing someone who knew someone—even then, you could consider yourself pretty lucky. Allen Terdiman, now a doctor in New York, was only thirteen in 1945, but he vividly remembers going aboard a luxury train at Pennsylvania Station:

136

My younger brother was quite ill and had to be taken to a warm climate. It was wartime, but through a connection, my aunt was able to book him and my mother into a stateroom of the *Broadway Limited*. I was filled with anticipation, walking through that great train shed and descending the steps to the train platform. I remember how excited I was to see the elegant interior of the train. My mother and brother were going to be gone for six months, but I wasn't sad. In that station, all emotions seemed to be suspended and there was this wonderful sense of occasion even when the reason to be there wasn't a happy one. When the train pulled out with my brother and my mother on it, I suddenly felt the loss of them. I remember that snow was falling outside. It was a cold, dreary day, but I hadn't noticed it until we left Pennsylvania Station and walked outside.

As the war intensified, many wounded soldiers coming off ships were transferred to hospital trains that passed through Pennsylvania Station. Al-

Soldiers wait in the concourse during the summer of 1942.

137

though the Red Cross was no longer responsible for providing food and medical supplies to the armed forces on troop trains as it had done during World War I, the organization did serve coffee and doughnuts at ports of embarkation and whenever hospital trains were delayed. In New York the Red Cross Ship Service saw troops off and welcomed them home, an activity that spilled over into Pennsylvania Station.

For the Pennsylvania Railroad the war was a time of incredible activity. New York City opened its arms to servicemen who wanted a few days of relaxation before returning to bases, shipping out overseas, or going home on leave. Soldiers, sailors, marines, and fliers poured in and out of the station every day. Traffic on the New York–Washington line, in particular, increased dramatically, since Washington was of course the nation's nerve center and many of the military training camps were located in the Southeast. Prior to the war the peak day's travel over the Philadelphia–Washington line occurred in 1937, on the occasion of Roosevelt's second inauguration, when 68,000 people boarded trains from Pennsylvania Station. On December 24, 1943, over two and a half times that many tickets—178,892 to be exact— were collected.

All this activity contributed to a resurgence of health for the Pennsylvania Railroad. The price of its stock rose from seventeen dollars to a high of forty-seven, and by 1942 the railroad was able to pay its stockholders a dividend of five dollars per share. Although both the Pennsylvania Railroad and its competitor, the New York Central, profited from the war and emerged from it in sound financial shape, the New York Central used its assets to put its balance sheets in order, concentrating on liquidity while ignoring needed track repair and replenishment of its rolling stock. The Pennsy, in contrast, was a strong company before the war and in 1945 was confident enough in its future to purchase nearly four hundred passenger coaches. Its freight business was doing very well and was seemingly immune to competition from other carriers. The railroad that was still the leading carrier of people in the country saw no reason why its passenger service could not compete effectively with buses and automobiles. Airplanes were still considered exotic machines used only by the brave or the eccentric, and car production had all but come to a halt during the war. During the darkest days of the Depression people had ridden the silver supertrains across the continent. There was every reason to believe that when the war was over, passengers would again flock to the train stations.

On August 15, 1945, crowds began to gather in Times Square, their eyes focused on the band of electric lights that circled the *Times* building. After a week of rumor thousands waited into early evening to see if the rumor would become fact. At 7:03 P.M. the band of letters spelled out: OFFICIAL—TRUMAN ANNOUNCES JAPANESE SURRENDER.

In May of that year, a somewhat more sedate crowd had gathered in the same place to celebrate V–E Day, marking the end of the war in Europe. But the country then was still fighting Japan, a fact that tempered celebration. With Japan's surrender, it was all over at last. Cheering strangers hugged one another. The crowds spilled down Broadway, along side streets, and finally into Pennsylvania Station. In the concourse, where so many of them had once said their good-byes, soldiers and sailors tossed their hats into the air and danced in circles.

New York City was an endless celebration. The faces of women glistened with tears; the days of waiting and terrible uncertainty were finally over. On the faces of soldiers and sailors was relief, an exhausted calm beneath the revelry. But further inside, behind the sense of relief, was a need for change, a desire to put the past behind them and find new lives. They had returned from the outer limits of hell, the President who had led them through was now dead, and the monster who had done most to create the inferno was dead, too. No one wanted to look over his shoulder at where he had been. GI Joe was interested in tomorrow. He was going to marry his girl and whisk her off to a place of calm and innocence and new beginnings.

It was called the suburbs. On Long Island, in some old potato fields, William Levitt was building a whole town of cottages with gardens and fresh air. The big city was no place to raise a family. And if living in Levittown meant that the new American family was no longer in a place where everything was close at hand, buying a car would solve that. In the year 1938, on the eve of the war, two million automobiles were sold. In 1950 the figure was over six and a half million and increasing. The auto industry was not able to keep up with the demand.

It was a time of endless promise, a time when people felt that in order to embrace the new they had to turn their backs on the old. Things that held yesterday's memories were shunned or ignored. For Pennsylvania Station the days of its brief, emotion-filled life were numbered.

The terrific press of wartime traffic inevitably meant delayed trains. Here servicemen heading back to their bases crowd the stationmaster's office to receive the late slips that will prove their tardiness is legitimate.

Overleaf: During the war the station was one of the busiest places in America. In 1945 alone, one hundred and nine million people passed through it.
MARJORY COLLINS

139

CHAPTER FIFTEEN

THE END OF PENNSYLVANIA STATION

The death knell was so muffled that few heard it. Back in 1944 Congress had passed the Federal Highway Act, providing for $1.5 million for building roads once the war was over. Not long after the Victory Day celebrations ended, work on the new superhighways began. In 1946 New Jersey started building its turnpike, which would stretch from the Hudson all the way to Pennsylvania. In July of that year New York State began building its thruway, connecting New York City to Buffalo.

In 1945, at the close of the war, three out of every four people who traveled between cities took a train, while only three out of every hundred took a plane. Ten years later, the situation had changed drastically. The train and the airplane were in a nearly neck-and-neck race, with one-third of passengers riding trains while one-quarter took planes. When the war ended, all the technology the aviation industry mastered in battle was quickly applied to commercial travel. The small unpredictable machine that flew only when weather conditions were ideal had grown into a sleek, dependable airplane. The tiny, two-engine propeller craft of the late thirties had been replaced by planes like the DC-6, which flew from coast to coast, day and night, in less than seven hours.

It became apparent that the day when the railroads were the prime movers of people was over. That day would have come even sooner had the Depression and World War II not stifled automobile production. There were practical reasons for people to drive their cars on short hops and take a plane for longer journeys. But beyond the practical was the emotional. In the 1950s Americans were headstrong lovers, romancing their flashy new cars and venturing willingly into the clouds. Trains, with their evocation of sentimental journeys, tugged at memory, carrying people back into a past they were eager to forget.

The Pennsylvania Railroad's balance sheets reflected the national mood. The railroad that had come out of the war in sound shape was now operating with a deficit that by 1951 reached nearly seventy-two million dollars. Everyone knew this was no mere slump. Railroading was in trouble, and steps would have to be taken if it was to stay on the tracks. The railroad cut back on services: poorly traveled routes were eliminated, and what money there was to spend went into runs that were showing a profit. In this cost-

*With Cassatt and McKim and their era long dead, the station began, in the
1950s, to suffer the gradual erosion of its great, clean vistas. In 1956 this
counter, designed to increase ticket sales, went up in the main waiting room.
Its negligible beauty was further diminished by the fact that it blocked
off the entrance to the concourse.*

cutting frenzy it was inevitable that the panic-stricken railroad would turn to its prized station to see how it could produce more revenue.

As early as 1951 the Pennsylvania Railroad discussed plans to sell the air rights to some of its property near the station for a proposed world trade center. The area in question was above the tracks between Ninth and Tenth avenues. The trade center idea fizzled, but it started the wheels in motion. Each year thereafter, another proposal to develop Pennsylvania Railroad property surfaced until finally, in December 1954, the real estate firm of Webb and Knapp purchased an option for the development of air rights, not over the tracks at Ninth and Tenth avenues but between Seventh and Eighth avenues, where Pennsylvania Station itself stood. A year later, in June 1955, the station's fate was sealed when James Symes, Pennsy president, and William Zeckendorf, president of Webb and Knapp, signed an agreement to sell the air rights and build a new station below street level.

Not a word of this leaked to the public. New Yorkers were not told that the station, given to them as a gift, the building designed to last forever, was about to be taken away. Any suspicions they might have entertained that the railroad would sell its station were probably allayed by the act of vandalism that was about to take place.

In 1956, a year after the agreement was signed, architect Lester C. Tichey designed an enormous ticket counter to be erected in the main waiting room. The whole enterprise, with television monitors on which people could watch their reservations being made, seemed to be an attempt to create the ambience of a small airline terminal within the station.

Whatever the intention, the reality was an ugly saw-toothed clamshell. The huge glowing monstrosity that was supposed to introduce modern convenience sat in the center of the main waiting room, permanently blocking access from its main doors to the concourse. In order to accommodate the clerks who manned the new ticket counter, both the ladies' and the men's waiting rooms were removed, and in a half-hearted gesture to the comfort of passengers who would no longer have anyplace to sit, the railroad installed a few benches in the concourse. To reach these, passengers were forced to take a labyrinthine path along the north and south sides of the main waiting room. It was also during this time that automobile displays, fluorescent-lighted advertisements, and flashy glass-and-steel storefronts invaded the station.

In May 1960, at its annual stockholders meeting, the Pennsylvania Railroad announced that a detailed engineering study had been completed with the purpose of possibly developing the air rights over Pennsylvania Station. This, five years *after* just such an agreement had been signed between the president of the railroad and Webb and Knapp! Stockholders were told that the station was in terrible shape and operated at a loss of $1.5 million each year. During that same year, 1960, the Madison Square Garden Corporation was formed and began putting together the package it planned to sell to the public.

All the while, Pennsylvania Station went about the business of receiving and discharging the passengers that flowed in and out of sixty-four long-distance trains and the Long Island Railroad. But things had changed. The number of redcaps had been cut almost in half. People coming off trains now had to search for someone to help them with their baggage. A film of dirt had crept over the entire building, from the stately interior to the outside walls. Most people who knew the station only as it was now would have been surprised to learn that what grime had made to seem an ugly gray granite was really sparkling pink. Phil Donnelly, a train dispatcher for AMTRAK, remembered the station during its last years and saw a psychological reason why people were willing to let it be destroyed: "The station was grimy on the outside, and there was a certain monotony about the exterior along the sides. Perhaps this building that now resembled a mausoleum reminded people on some level that the age of railroads was gone and it made them nervous to have this relic here, reminding them of something that no longer lived."

Months went by without mention of the railroad's plans for the station. On November 27, 1960, Pennsylvania Station turned fifty years old. A half-century before, one hundred thousand New Yorkers had thronged in to gasp at its beauty. Now the great building was ignored. There was no fanfare, no announcements by the railroad. Indeed it would have been an odd celebration, considering that the company was now in the process of trying to tear the station down.

On July 21, 1961, the Pennsylvania finally went public with its plans. An article in the *New York Times* spoke mostly of the new Madison Square Garden complex that would rise atop the station. Much was said of the need for a new sports complex, but nothing was mentioned about the fact that the station would have to be sacrificed. In fact, according to the article the main waiting room was to remain intact, and the complex was to be built around it.

Six days later another article appeared, this one accompanied by an artist's rendering of the new station, which looked like a set design for a science fiction movie. Buried in the middle of that article was the news that Pennsylvania Station was to be destroyed. Barclay Johnson, a former vice president of Gibbs & Hill, Inc., the company that was responsible for the station's construction, said recently, "The guys who planned it . . . who sold it to the Madison Square Garden people, did their work very well. They kept it a deep, dark secret until they got the wrecking crew there."

As for the Pennsylvania Railroad, the deal they made with the Madison Square Garden Corporation was dazzling. In return for its air rights, the railroad got a smaller, modernized station and a quarter interest in the Madison Square Garden complex. Like a gambler selling off his family heirlooms to back the next roll of the dice, the railroad did not realize that this trade-off, however generous the terms, would fail to save it from its eventual dissolution. The end was in sight.

The Pennsylvania Railroad's timing could not have been better—for its purposes. Even though the railroad knew that the structure it intended to destroy was an historic edifice, it also knew that nowhere was there a bureau, federal or local, that could prevent its destruction. In 1960 there was no Landmarks Preservation Commission. The City Planning Commission could rule only on what was going up, not on what was coming down, and the public seemed no longer interested in the soot-laden tomb that had sat for more than half a century on eight of its city blocks. It *was* interested in

Overleaf: More harbingers of the station's impending destruction—at left, soda machines and advertising clutter have invaded the arcade; at right, beyond the statue of Pennsylvania president Samuel Rea, a glass box sells Barricini candy.

the shiny, modernistic architecture of tomorrow, and that is precisely what the Madison Square Garden Corporation promised.

Those few who did care—the six young architects who had formed AGBANY, the ad hoc organization to save the station, and a handful of others—tried in vain to sound the alarm. In 1961 they appealed to Mayor Robert Wagner to have a landmarks commission formed. A year later a commission was appointed, but it was not until 1965, two years after the station's destruction, that the commission had any power to act. Meanwhile the American Institute of Architects protested, as did the Municipal Art Society. Editorials defending the station appeared in newspapers, but the railroad knew it had won. "We thought we were talking to other people," Philip Johnson said as he recalled picketing with the other architects in front of Penn Station on that August day in 1962. "We were really only talking to each other."

It was not until the station was leveled, until the Great Room and the concourse had vanished, that New Yorkers began to realize what they had lost. Still, the lesson was slow to be learned, and, consequently, other old buildings were brought down. "We marched twenty years ago," said Johnson. "It took that amount of time before the citizens of the city were completely converted."

Time was not on the side of Pennsylvania Station. Perhaps its roots, planted so firmly in the glorious days of the Roman Empire, could not allow it to survive in the more mundane soil of America. Lewis Mumford has written, "There is never too much of that grand Roman quality in a modern city," and certainly Charles McKim would have agreed with him. But, according to some critics, it was that Roman quality that may have distanced Pennsylvania Station from the affections of some people. "It was templelike in that it was inaccessible," the chairman of the New York Landmarks Conservancy, Brendan Gill, told me. "The feeling when you approached it was awe and intimidation." Gill spoke of the carriage ramps looking at times like dark, mysterious tunnels. "Those car ramps inside the mammoth pillars set the building off from the neighborhood." One could always argue, however, that it was this mysterious quality, so rare in the architecture of New York City, that made the carriage ramps unique and appealing.

Inside the station, McKim's giant tribute to the Belle Epoque resulted in space that, although essentially functional and magnificent to the eye, could weary the body. This situation was discussed in 1916 by John Droege, a superintendent of the New York, New Haven and Hartford Railroad, who wrote: "The average traveler will be dumbfounded when he views the magnificent waiting room and concourse for the first time, but in more cases than a few the immensity of things and the magnificence will lose their luster when he has traversed the "magnificent distance" from the sidewalk to the train or *vice versa*. It cannot be denied that this is a disadvantage which was not overcome in the planning of the station."

That McKim had to design a station whose tracks were thirty-six feet below street level did not make his task easy. The station had also to accommodate two separate railroads, one a long-distance line and the other a commuter line, each feeding from opposite directions. Added to these problems, the subway system was expanding while the station was under

construction, and both the Eighth and Seventh Avenue lines would have stops there. As a result the station was built on three levels: one for tracks and train platforms, another for subway lines and the Long Island Railroad concourse and ticket offices, and a third for the general concourse and main waiting room. All of these levels were below the street, producing a cavernous, sometimes confusing pattern of walkways, exit ramps, and staircases.

Beyond these design problems were others McKim introduced himself. With his reverence for Roman grandeur, he sometimes sacrificed convenience to the drama of great space. The waiting room had no central information desk, as does Grand Central Station, where it serves not only as a convenience but as a focal point, bringing the rest of the elements in the room together. Indeed, the need for an information desk was so keenly felt that an octagonal one was later installed. The segregated auxiliary waiting rooms, while high on civility, did nothing to inspire warmth and conviviality, since men and women were not only separated by distance but by walls as well. The formal dining room, with the great sweep of space that appealed to the sensibilities of turn-of-the-century New York, in later years felt cold and institutional as New Yorkers embraced the comfortable and informal.

Philip Johnson, who fought to save the station and who has confessed a deep affection for the building's Roman lineage, nevertheless conceded that some features of McKim's grand design were unduly overwhelming. "There's no sense in doubling up the concourse," Johnson said, referring to the separate exit concourse below the great steel and glass train shed. "And all those great empty spaces. The vast dining room—it wasn't well thought out." Paul Goldberger, the architecture critic for the *New York Times* and a great admirer of Pennsylvania Station, agrees with Johnson that the use of space is more expeditious in Grand Central Terminal. "Grand Central has that extraordinary natural procession, where you get off a train and all you do is walk," Goldberger told me. "Penn Station was never as natural and simple a thing as Grand Central." But again, it was never meant to be: McKim was not concerned with economy of space when he carried the passenger from the dramatic train shed through the elegant main

Less than half a century after the McKim, Mead and White drawings appeared in the Times, *architects were making renderings of a new Pennsylvania Station.*

149

"When completed," Pennsylvania president James M. Symes said bravely in 1955, "the new station will be the world's finest." And here it is: a bleak parody of railroad stations in general and a tragic joke in comparison with its magnificent predecessor.

waiting room and then through the arcade. He wanted to give his passenger time to adjust to the exciting city across the station's vestibule, to ease his way so that when he passed beyond the great Doric columns he would feel himself the city's invited guest.

Perhaps the more significant liability of the station was its location, considered by several architects and historians to have been too far from the city's heart. The single advantage of the site may have been its proximity to the Hudson River. Brendan Gill spoke with me about the time when ferries and ocean liners dotted the river. "When the railroad came under the river, the railroad traffic itself was at its height. There was a lot of activity. One wanted to go over there [to the site of the station]. There were ocean liners coming and going. I'm sure when it was built the exuberance of being in an expanding city, of coming across on the water, was thrilling."

By the 1960s traffic on the Hudson had dwindled as trucks replaced the freighters that once brought much of the produce to the Northeast, and the luxury liners had vanished. When the river ceased to draw New Yorkers to its shores, there was little reason to travel to the West Side. The department stores along Herald Square, which had inspired the hopes of real estate people when Penn Station was rising, never did affect the use of the facility.

The length of a city block made all the difference: to the north and south of the station were furrier showrooms, a Catholic church, some bars, and a Greyhound bus terminal. On its western border was the post office, "a dam" said Gill "holding back the city, saying, 'I defy you to spill into the Hudson River.' "

There was little intermingling between the station and its disparate neighbors, which is not the case with Grand Central Terminal. Today, Grand Central is a hub in one of the most dynamic areas of the city. It serves as a passageway from one block to another. Its restaurant and shopping facilities are used daily by people who never catch a train from the terminal. It would be difficult to imagine Forty-second Street without Grand Central. Penn Station, on the other hand, was on the edge of nowhere. One used it only to catch a train, and even then it meant going to a part of town that seemed removed from the rest of the city. To people who never had reason to take a train from it, Penn Station became an abstraction, something they knew was there but that never really existed for them.

There were all these things: timing, location, the intimidating Roman facade made gloomy by dirt, the great stretches of space inside. All of them made it easier for an ailing railroad to rid itself of its costly burden. "I knew that it was run-down, that the dining room was no good, and the waste of space was enormous," Philip Johnson said. "But I didn't see at that time— and I still don't—why it made any difference. We have to live with our past, and Penn Station was a great example of it. The main reason we marched that day was to protest the losing of an urban jewel."

Like Fabergé's imperial treasures, Pennsylvania Station was fashioned at a particular time when the resources to build it were at hand. An opening in the financial clouds at the turn of the century gave Alexander Cassatt the momentum to build it. If he had waited another ten years, he would never have been able to accumulate the land on which it rested. The resources to bring together the tons of Italian marble and delicate pink granite, the craftsmanship to construct the intricate arched steel dome of the concourse, the vision and the generosity of spirit to build a temple that would delight man's soul, belonged to another time. Cassatt conceived his railroad station as a landmark and built it to last through centuries. Yet, after a mere fifty years, the shortsighted acts of desperate men and the indifference of a sleeping city brought it down.

"It was extraordinary architecture," Paul Goldberger said. "It was a remarkable balance of the monumental and the very basically functional. It was a sensible building on every possible level. It was also an extraordinary symbol. And there was no contradiction between its role as a symbol and its function. I think maybe that was the greatest achievement of all."

"I miss the station very much," said Philip Johnson. "Every time I take a train to Philadelphia I remember it. I've been saying this all along . . . the city deserves a great entranceway." Cassatt and McKim would have agreed. Now anyone who wants to connect with Alexander Cassatt's dream and Charles McKim's vision of a great railroad station for a great city will have to look for it in books. The station that they had dreamed about and built, the station that grew out of the power of the railroads and, more important, out of man's desire to express his spirit in stone, is gone forever.

An earthbound eagle outside Madison Square Garden is all that remains to remind us of the act of civic vandalism that swept away the great station that once stood there.

BILL DIEHL

In 1982 the Morosco Theater followed Pennsylvania Station into eternity.

EPILOGUE

Five years after the station's destruction, the debt-ridden Pennsylvania Railroad merged with the New York Central to form the Penn-Central. Two years after that, in 1970, the Penn-Central declared bankruptcy.

In 1981 Madison Square Garden Corporation, citing losses of eight million dollars that year, asked the city of New York to help. If something were not done quickly, the Rangers and the Knicks would be forced to abandon New York for another sports arena in New Jersey—one built on landfill from the rubble of Pennsylvania Station.

In March 1982 New York City agreed to cut Madison Square Garden's real estate taxes by 75 percent, a loss to the city of nearly three million dollars a year. By the summer of 1982 Governor Hugh Carey signed a bill providing a tax break totaling fifty million dollars for the Garden. He also agreed to subsidize its energy costs. These concessions were part of a ten-year contract between New York City and Gulf & Western, owners of Madison Square Garden, to keep the Rangers and the Knicks in New York.

Two years after the contract was signed, on January 8, 1984, a front-page headline in the *Daily News* read: LAST HURRAH FOR THE GARDEN? OWNER WANTS TO KNOCK IT DOWN. Citing revenue losses of more than two million dollars a year, Gulf & Western now wants to raze Madison Square Garden and replace it with an office building. According to Gulf & Western officials, the complex has failed to show a profit since it opened in 1968, and replacing it with an office building would likely make a handsome profit.

History repeats itself. When the Madison Square Garden Corporation informed New Yorkers it was going to replace their magnificent railroad station with a sports complex, the same tired arguments defending the plan were pulled out: the added tax revenues for the city, the boost to the construction industry, and the need for that particular building in that particular place.

A few years later the snake oil salesmen were back, promising to revitalize the shabby Times Square area. The victim in this sleight of hand was the magnificent Astor Hotel, on Broadway between Forty-fourth and Forty-fifth streets, replaced by an office building. Times Square continued to deteriorate despite the Astor's removal, and whenever the office building had trouble renting space, its location was given as a reason it could not draw tenants.

153

As this book was being written another larger-than-life building was rising across the street from where the Astor Hotel once stood. Again the argument was handed to the public: this building will do what the office tower could not—it will revitalize Times Square. The price for this illusion has been costly to New Yorkers. Gone are the Morosco, Helen Hayes, and Bijou theaters, three fine, acoustically perfect houses with wonderful histories. Gone is the Pickwick Hotel, one of the few stable, charming hotels in the Times Square area affordable to most people who visit New York City. In place of these buildings will rise the glittery Marriott Marquis, a mountain of concrete that promises to dwarf the theaters that surround it and keep middle-class Americans out of its costly rooms.

We have lost so much to Progress. The magnificent Metropolitan Opera House that stood on Thirty-ninth Street and Broadway was destroyed, apparently for the most selfish of reasons: the Metropolitan Opera Association, fearing competition, insisted it be torn down when they sold it. Two splendid movie theaters, the Paramount and the Roxy (the "Cathedral of the Motion Picture") were ground to dust. The elegant Astor Hotel is gone. So is Pennsylvania Station.

These were essentially public buildings, built for the use of the citizens of this country. They should have been preserved, not only because they had architectural merit but because they belonged to us. In the flim-flam schemes designed to sell us things we do not always want, it is sometimes difficult to see how much is being taken from us. When the developers pack up and leave after making their deals, there is nothing left but the sense of betrayal and the knowledge that, in some way, we have been violated.

If Madison Square Garden is torn down soon, it will have lasted twenty years or less. What a sad and capricious epitaph for the railroad station that stood in its way.

When Pennsylvania Station was brought down, the *New York Times* wrote, in an October 30, 1963, editorial: "We will probably be judged not by the monuments we build but by those we have destroyed." History teaches. We have only to listen.

ACKNOWLEDGMENTS

When I began this book, I realized very quickly how little I knew about Pennsylvania Station. I had embarked on a journey that would take me into the separate worlds of architecture, railroading, and historic preservation, and like Tennessee Williams's Blanche DuBois, I would have to depend on the kindness of strangers to light my way. Lucky for me, those strangers who loved the station as I did were enormously generous with their time, stories, and their priceless memorabilia. It astounded me how unhesitatingly people entrusted me with irreplaceable books, photographs, and architectural maps and drawings, many dating back to the turn of the century. Some of those strangers are now good friends. I must thank the railroaders Philip A. Donnelly, George Keegan, Barclay Johnson, and Ann Williams and, most of all, Francis Meaney, Jr., for guiding me through a world that had been alien to me. George Flatow, a ninety-seven-year-old former Pennsylvania Railroad employee who saw the station rise and a half-century later watched it come down, provided me with memories and rare photographs. Architects Norman Jaffee, Norval White, Elliot Willensky, Peter Samton, and Philip Johnson all gave me their passionate memories of the lost battle to save the station. Kent Barwick, Paul Goldberger, Brendan Gill, and Geoffrey Platt explained the importance of preserving our landmarks far more eloquently than I could. Helena Zinkham of the New-York Historical Society and Steven Miller, Nancy Kessler-Post, and Jennifer Bright of the Museum of the City of New York accepted countless requests for photographs of Pennsylvania Station with goodwill and genial cooperation. My husband and daughter endured the great preoccupation with patience. And last but far from least, I must thank my editors, Barbara Ravage, who wanted the book as much as I did and guided me through the painstaking process of transforming an idea into print, Alan Axelrod, whose unfailing fine-tooth comb untangled the obscurities, Constance Roosevelt, Richard Snow, and Carla Davidson, who were there at the end of the line to give it the final push into print.

NOTES ON
THE SOURCES

During the course of preparing this book, I interviewed Norman Jaffe, Elliot Willensky, Norval White, Peter Samton, and Philip Johnson, all of whom were instrumental in trying to save Pennsylvania Station. Some of the conversations took place in their offices, and others over the telephone. Interviews with Geoffrey Platt, the first chairman of the Landmarks Preservation Commission, and Kent Barwick, who served as the commission's chairman while this book was being written, took place in their offices. Brendan Gill spoke with me on the telephone, and Paul Goldberger was interviewed at the *New York Times*. Alfred Eisenstaedt spent a morning with me in his office at *Life* magazine, looking over the photos he took in the station concourse during World War II and recalling his impressions. Archie Harris was interviewed in his office near Pennsylvania Station. Barclay Johnson spent an afternoon with me in his home recalling his days at Gibbs & Hill, Inc., whose offices were inside the old Pennsylvania Station. I interviewed Phil Donnelly in an office in the present Pennsylvania Station. Leonard Leader wrote to me about his memories of the station when he went off to war. Robert Riddell, now executive director of the USO, recalled in a telephone conversation his days working behind the information desk in the main waiting room, and Allen Terdiman spoke with me of his boyhood memories of walking through the *Broadway Limited*.

Pages   Source Notes

15   **"Just another job"**: *The New York Times*, October 29, 1963.

18   **"For here . . . distant roof"**: Thomas Wolfe, *You Can't Go Home Again* (New York: Charles Scribner's Sons, 1940), p. 48.

26   **"a West . . . reconstruction"**: Lewis Mumford, "The Pennsylvania Station Nightmare," in *The Highway and the City* (New York: Harcourt Brace & World, Inc., 1963), p. 148.

28   **"You realize . . . nobly. . . . Fifty years . . . will protest"**: "Penn Pals," *Time* (August 10, 1962), 80:42.

32   **"I had . . . spoiled"**: Patricia T. Davis, *End of the Line* (New York: Neale Watson Academic Publications, Inc., 1978), p. 30.

35   **"They are . . . submarine tunnels"**: Samuel Rea, in U.S. Congress, House Committee on Commerce, *Bridge Across the Hudson River at New York City*, H. Rept. 928, 51st Cong., 1st sess., 1890, House Reports 3:19–22; CH; pp. 464–65.

36   **"I reached . . . our direction"**: Charles Moore, *The Life and Times of Charles Follen McKim* (Boston: Houghton Mifflin Co., 1929), p. 273.

36   **"a cramped . . . mean ugliness"**: Edith Wharton, *A Backward Glance* (1933; reprinted ed., New York: Charles Scribner's Sons, 1933) p. 55.

38   **"Lawrence Grant White . . . the axis"**: Charles C. Baldwin, *Stanford White* (New York: Dodd, Mead & Company, Inc., 1931), pp. 115–116.

38   **"sound judgement . . . the storms"**: Lawrence Grant White quoted by Leland M. Roth, "McKim, Mead and White Reappraised," in reprint ed. of McKim, Mead and White, *A Monograph of the Works of McKim, Mead and White, 1879–1915* (New York: Benjamin Blom, 1973) p. 13.

39   **"Let me . . . rebuild it"**: Moore, *McKim*, p. 205.

39   **"Each building . . . event"**: Moore, *McKim*, p. 55.

40   **"His wife's . . . hearse"**: Edith Wharton, *The Age of Innocence* (1920; reprint ed., New York: Charles Scribner's Sons, 1968), p. 284.

42   **"Everybody . . . bisquits"**: Davis, *End of the Line*, p. 163.

50   **"an institution . . . man's life"**: Jacques Barzun, as quoted in Joseph R. Daughen and Peter Binzen, *The Wreck of the Penn Central* (Boston: Little, Brown & Co., 1971), p. 43.

71   **"Put the road . . . to live"**: Richard O'Connor, *Hell's Kitchen*, (Philadelphia and New York: J.B. Lippincott Company, 1958) p. 13.

82   **"To Mr. McKim . . . good taste"**: Moore, *McKim*, p. 58.

83   **"as being . . . of prayer"**: Baldwin, *Stanford White*, p. 302.

89   **"Her loss . . . her death"**: Davis, *End of the Line*, p. 179.

103   **"whose foresight . . . New York City"**: *The History of the Engineering Construction and Equipment of the Pennsylvania Railroad Company's New York Terminal and Approaches* (New York: Isaac H. Blanchard Company, 1912), p. 19.

120   **"There Polish . . . permanent crew"**: "The Pennsylvania Station," *Fortune* (July 1939), p. 132.

123   **"As we . . . forever bright"**: "A Postcard Message from a Soldier: 'Passing Through Pennsylvania Station,'" in American Red Cross, New York Chapter, *Annual Report, 1919–1920.*

125   **"In the . . . through it . . ."**: William Faulkner, "Pennsylvania Station," in *Collected Stories of William Faulkner* (New York: Random House, 1950), p. 609.

148   **"There is . . . modern city"**: Mumford, "The Pennsylvania Station Nightmare," p. 146.

148   **"The average . . . the station"**: John A. Droege, *Passenger Terminals and Trains* (1916; reprint ed., Milwaukee: Kalmbach Publishing Co., 1974), p. 157.

BIBLIOGRAPHY

Books

Alexander, Edwin P. *On the Main Line*. New York: Clarkson N. Potter, Inc., 1971.

American Society of Civil Engineers. *Transactions of the American Society of Civil Engineers*. Vol. 69. New York: 1910.

Andrews, Wayne. *Architecture, Ambition and Americans*. New York: Harper & Row, Inc., 1955.

———. *The Vanderbilt Legend*. New York: Harcourt Brace and Company, 1941.

Baldwin, Charles C. *Stanford White*. New York: Dodd, Mead & Company, 1931.

Beebe, Lucius. *Mr. Pullman's Elegant Palace Cars*. New York: Doubleday & Co., Inc., 1961.

Beebe, Lucius, and Charles Clegg. *The Trains We Rode*. Two vols. Berkeley: Howell-North Books, 1965.

Bendiner, Robert. *Just Around the Corner*. New York: Harper & Row, Inc., 1967.

Bezilla, Michael. *Electric Traction on the Pennsylvania Railroad: 1895–1968*. University Park: Pennsylvania State University Press, 1980.

Bird, Caroline. *The Invisible Scar*. New York: David McKay Co., Inc., 1966.

Burnham, Alan. *New York Landmarks*. Middletown, Conn.: Wesleyan University Press, 1963.

Condit, Carl W. *The Port of New York: A History of the Rail and Terminal Systems from the Beginnings to Pennsylvania Station*. Vol. 1. Chicago: University of Chicago Press, 1980.

———. *The Port of New York: A History of the Rail and Terminal System from the Grand Central Electrification to the Present*. Vol. 2. Chicago: University of Chicago Press, 1980.

Cudahy, Brian J. *Rails Under the Mighty Hudson*. Brattleboro, Vt.: Stephen Greene Press, 1975.

———. *Under the Sidewalks of New York: The Story of the Greatest Subway System in the World*. Brattleboro, Vt.: Stephen Greene Press, 1979.

Daughen, Joseph R., and Peter Binzen. *The Wreck of the Penn Central*. Boston: Little, Brown & Co., 1971.

Davis, Patricia T. *End of the Line*. New York: Neale Watson Academic Publications, Inc., 1978.

Droege, John A. *Passenger Terminals and Trains*. 1916; reprint ed., Milwaukee: Kalmbach Publishing Co., 1974.

Faulkner William. "Pennsylvania Station." In *Collected Stories of William Faulkner*. New York: Random House, 1950.

Fischler, Stan. *Uptown, Downtown*. New York: Hawthorn Books, Inc., 1976.

Freidel, Frank B. *America in the Twentieth Century.* New York: Alfred A. Knopf Inc., 1960.

Gibbs & Hill, Inc. *Before the Colors Fade: A Personal History of Gibbs & Hill, Inc.* New York: Gibbs & Hill, Inc., 1975.

Goldstone, Harmon H., and Martha Dalyrmple. *History Preserved: A Guide to New York City Landmarks and Historic Districts.* New York: Simon & Schuster, Inc., 1974.

Granger, Alfred Hoyt. *Charles Follen McKim: A Study of His Life and Work.* Boston: Houghton Mifflin Co., Inc., 1913.

Greiff, Constance M. *Lost America.* Princeton, N.J.: Pyne Press, 1971.

Grow, Lawrence. *Waiting for the 5:05.* New York: Universe Books, 1977.

Hornung, Clarence P. *The American Eagle in Art and Design.* New York: Dover Publishing, 1978.

Hadas, Moses, and the editors of Time-Life Books. *Imperial Rome.* New York: Time-Life Books, 1965.

Hungerford, Edward. *Men and Iron: A History of the New York Central.* New York: Thomas Y. Crowell Company, 1938.

Isaacson, Philip M. *The American Eagle.* Boston: New York Graphic Society, 1975.

Jensen, Oliver. *The American Heritage History of Railroads in America.* New York: American Heritage Publishing Co., Inc., 1975.

Lane, Wheaton J. *Commodore Vanderbilt: An Epic of the Steam Age.* New York: Alfred A. Knopf, Inc., 1942.

Loewy, Raymond. *Never Leave Well Enough Alone.* New York: Simon and Schuster, 1951.

Marshall, David. *Grand Central.* New York: McGraw-Hill Book Company, Inc., 1946.

Mayer, Grace M. *Once Upon a City.* New York: The Macmillan Company, 1958.

Moody, John. *The Railroad Builders.* New Haven: Yale University Press, 1919.

Mooney, Michael Macdonald. *Evelyn Nesbit and Stanford White: Love and Death in the Gilded Age.* New York: William Morrow and Company, Inc., 1976.

Moore, Charles. *The Life and Times of Charles Follen McKim.* Boston and New York: Houghton Mifflin Co., 1929.

Mumford, Lewis. "The Pennsylvania Station Nightmare." In *The Highway and the City.* New York: Harcourt Brace & World, Inc., 1963.

———. *Roots of Contemporary American Architecture.* New York: Reinhold Publishing Co., 1952.

O'Connor, Richard. *Hell's Kitchen.* Philadelphia and New York: J.B. Lippincott Company, 1958.

Ogburn, Charlton. *Railroads: The Great American Adventure.* Washington, D.C.: Prepared by the Special Publications Division, National Geographic Society, 1977.

Pennsylvania Railroad Company. *Centennial History of the Pennsylvania Railroad Company: 1846–1946.* Philadelphia: Pennsylvania Railroad Company, 1949.

Pennsylvania Railroad Company. *The History of the Engineering Construction and Equipment of the Pennsylvania Railroad Company's New York Terminal and Approaches.* New York: Isaac H. Blanchard Company, 1912.

Reed, Henry Hope, Jr. *The Golden City.* New York: Doubleday & Co., Inc., 1959.

Roth, Leland M. *The Architecture of McKim, Mead & White: 1870–1920.* New York: Garland Publishing Co., Inc., 1978.

———. "McKim, Mead and White Reappraised," in reprint ed. of McKim, Mead and White, *A Monograph of the Works of McKim, Mead and White.* New York: Benjamin Blom, 1973.

Silver, Nathan. *Lost New York.* Boston: Houghton Mifflin, 1967.

Sobel, Robert. *The Fallen Colossus*. New York: Weybright and Talley, 1977.

Stone, Jill. *Times Square: A Pictorial History*. New York: Collier Books, 1982.

Tharp, Louise Hall. *Saint-Gaudens and the Gilded Era*. Boston: Little, Brown, 1969.

Westing, Fred. *Penn Station: Its Tunnels and Side Rodders*. Seattle: Superior Publishing Company, 1978.

Wharton, Edith. *The Age of Innocence*. 1920; reprint ed., New York: Charles Scribner's Sons, 1968.

————. *A Backward Glance*. 1934; reprint ed., New York: Charles Scribner's Sons, 1964.

Whitaker, Rogers E. *All Aboard with E. M. Frimbo, World's Greatest Railroad Buff*. New York: Grossman Publishers, 1974.

Wolfe, Thomas. *You Can't Go Home Again*. New York: Charles Scribner's Sons, 1940.

Periodicals and Pamphlets

"AGBANY Asks and the Mayor Promises: Action on Penn Station." *Architectural Record* (October 1962), 117:9.

"AGBANY Proposes Plan to Save Penn Station." *Progressive Architecture* (January 1963), 44:48.

"AGBANY vs. Apathy at Penn Station." *Architectural Forum* (September 1962), 117:5.

"Architects Want Penn Station Saved." *Architectural Record* (September 1962), 132:23.

Editorial Announcements, item: "Pennsylvania Railroad." *Railroad Gazette* (November 22, 1889), 21:772.

Macrorie, Ken. "Arriving and Departing." *The Reporter* (September 13, 1962), 27:52–55.

"Penn Pals." *Time* (August 10, 1962), 80:42.

"Pennsylvania Station's Last Stand." *Architectural Forum* (February, 1963), 118:11.

Pennsylvania Railroad Company. *Pennsylvania Station in New York City* (commemorative booklet). Pennsylvania Railroad Company, 1910.

"Raising a New Garden: Air Space over Penn Station." *Business Week* (February 23, 1963), 142.

PERMISSIONS

INDEX